ALL YOU NEED TO KNOW ABOUT THE BIBLE

Book 6: enjoy your Bible!

BRIAN H EDWARDS

DayOne

ISBN 978-1-84625-589-2

British Library Cataloguing in Publication Data available

Published by Day One Publications
Ryelands Road, Leominster, HR6 8NZ
Telephone 01568 613 740 Fax 01568 611 473
North America Toll Free 888 329 6630
email—sales@dayone.co.uk
web site—www.dayone.co.uk

Cover design by Kathryn Chedgzoy
Printed by TJ International

ALL YOU NEED TO KNOW ABOUT THE BIBLE

BRIAN H EDWARDS

Book 6
Enjoy your Bible!

The series outline

Book 1 Can we trust it?

What this book is all about

1. **What's the Bible all about?**
   The Master Plan with Jesus Christ as the theme
2. **Remarkable prophecy**
   What do we do with these incredible predictions?
3. **Evidence of an eyewitness**
   Proof that the writers were there
4. **Did Jesus really live?**
   Jesus fixed in history
5. **Living letters for living churches**
   Marks of real letters to real Christians
6. **Fact or fiction?**
   Evidence of the Old Testament written in its time

Book 2 Big claims from a unique book

1. **The God who reveals himself**
   Evidence everywhere
2. **Ultimate truth**
   God-given and without error
3. **Jesus and his Bible**
   What Scriptures did Jesus use?
4. **The apostles and their Bible**
   What Scriptures did the apostles use?
5. **Absolute authority**
   Big claims by prophets, Jesus, and apostles
6. **Is the Bible enough?**
   Sufficient and final
7. **The Chicago statement**
   The inerrancy statement of the International Council for Biblical Inerrancy

Book 3 Have we got the right books?

1. **Who thought of a Bible?**
   The idea of a collection of books
2. **The Jews and their Bible**
   The books in the Old Testament
3. **The early Christians and their Bible**
   The beginning of a New Testament
4. **A growing collection**
   The development of the accepted books
5. **A complete New Testament**
   The books accepted across the Christian world
6. **Who wrote the books?**
   The writers of the New Testament books
7. **Helpful letters not in the Bible**
   More instructions for the young churches
8. **A library of lies**
   The writings of the heretics

Appendix
A chart of the church Fathers

Book 4 A journey from then to now

1. **From flames to fame**
   The story of the English Bible
2. **How old is the Old Testament?**
   The earliest copies
3. **How old is the New Testament?**
   The earliest copies
4. **Discovering the best text**
   Why are some verses different?
5. **Which translation?**
   The dilemma of many versions

Book 5 Sense as well as faith

Book 6 Enjoy your Bible!

Contents

What this book is all about

Three thousand years ago the psalmist wrote, 'I will walk about in freedom, for I have sought out your precepts...Your word is a lamp to my feet and a light for my path' (Psalm 119:45,105).

In the first book of this series, the Master plan of the Bible was outlined—how the books all fit together towards one great theme which is Jesus Christ the rescuer from sin. The second book emphasized the importance of biblical authority and what is meant by the 'sufficiency' of Scripture. From there the series unfolds the story of our English Bible, how we can be sure that we have the right text, how to choose a translation, and some of the best evidence for trusting its accuracy so that our commitment to Biblical inerrancy is unashamedly 'sense as well as faith.'

Most Christians want to read the Bible regularly, and in this book, various ways for this are suggested. There is nothing better than travelling through the whole Bible regularly, so that we are reminded of the great and small events, all of which contribute to the unfolding plan of salvation. However, there are rules to help us understand the Bible. They are essential, but not difficult. Two chapters will help us to read the Bible with common sense.

A number of easy-to-follow charts will enable us to get to grips with the narrative of the Bible. One lists the Old Testament books in their chronological order so that we can see where the prophets belong to the history. Another, pieces together the Gospel records of the life of Christ, and a third outlines the Acts of the Apostles and where the New Testament letters fit in. For those who would like to read through the entire Bible once in eighteen months—and significant parts of it twice—a chronological daily reading plan is offered. Brief notes show where each book fits into the unfolding story.

The ultimate purpose in reading the Bible is to draw us closer to God and fashion us more into the likeness of Jesus Christ, therefore the closing chapter of the whole series is entitled: 'Take time with God'. This suggests how we may plan our personal daily worship. The rush of modern life is only one reason for the loss of what used to be an essential feature for every Christian home. We have lost an appetite for prayer because it is no longer seen as the privilege it really is: when a forgiven sinner can approach boldly the immediate presence of the Sovereign God of the universe and call him 'Father'. His ever-listening ear is always open for the voice of his children. The Psalmist affirmed, 'O you who hear prayer, to you all men will come' (Psalm 65:2) and to this the Father responds, 'You will call upon me and come and pray to me, and I will listen to you (Jeremiah 29:12). This 'access to the Father' (Ephesians 2:18) is the greatest privilege of the Christian life.

Our time with God and his word is intended to be an enjoyable privilege. Let's make it so.

1. It's for you, it's alive—read it!

Few Christians would ever doubt the value of reading the Bible. However, where to start, what to expect from it and how to keep it up regularly are issues most face.

We need to read the Bible

The Bible is much more than a book of theology and history, although it is both. It is the voice of God speaking relevantly to every generation and in every culture. It is not a book for specialists and academics alone, but for ordinary people who want to know God's best way through the maze of life's complexities. Christians who believe the Bible is God's word for today are eager to read it and learn what God has to say.

'The word of God is living and active ... it judges the thoughts and attitudes of the heart' (Hebrews 4:12).

Repeatedly throughout Psalm 119 the psalmist tells us that he loves the law, rejoices in it, delights in it, longs for it, meditates on it, obeys it, and that it is the joy of his heart, sweet to his taste and far better than gold. He informs us how often he reads it, thinks about it and uses it: wherever he lodges (v. 54), in the night (v. 55), at midnight (v. 62), throughout the night (v. 148), throughout the day (v. 97), seven times a day (v. 164).

Few of us can match that. Fortunately, we are not expected to be bound by the legalism of reading the Bible seven times a day or at certain hours of the day. However, this godly man, writing possibly three thousand years ago, reveals just how precious should be this revelation of God to his people.

So, how best can we read the Bible?

We should read the Bible regularly and methodically

To get the best out of our Bible reading we should read it daily and with a plan, rather than dipping in and out randomly whenever we have a few spare moments. Perhaps, from what our psalmist has revealed to us, it may appear that he did precisely that: dip in and out at odd times. However, his 'odd times' seem to have included most of his day and night!

With so many English Bible translations and paraphrases available today, it will be helpful to read in this series Book 4 chapter 5 'Which translation?' For serious Bible study, a paraphrase is not good enough. The first essential is a translation that is as close to the original Hebrew and Greek text as can be obtained in a translation.

Once a good translation has been chosen, it is important to set aside some premium time; the length of time is not the most important condition, but the quiet, unhurried nature of the time is. We need to choose the best time of our day to be serious with God's word—not rushing it with the cereal in the morning, or as we drop exhausted into bed at the end of a tiring day. However, we may wish to close each day with what John Newton called his 'pillow verse'. A short reading or a single verse to settle our mind as we rest.

To help young children gain the idea of regular reading in the Bible, they may be introduced to one of the Bible translations especially translated for them. *The Jesus Storybook Bible* is suitable for children aged 5 to 11 inviting children to join in the greatest of all adventures and to discover for themselves that Jesus is at the centre of God's great story of salvation. Every narrative whispers his name. He is like the missing piece in a puzzle. The *New Century International Children's Bible* is suitable for the same age group. It claims to have been translated directly from the original texts into an English that can be read and understood by children aged between 6 and 12. It has large easy-to-read type in two columns and in short sentences and simple, modern vocabulary.

There are several ways in which we can read the Bible daily.

A SHORT PASSAGE WITH A BRIEF COMMENTARY

Some prefer to take only a few verses with a well-known commentator as a guide. There are many daily readings like this from reliable Bible teachers, both past and present.[1] That is an easy way in. It is attractive and undemanding. However, it doesn't take in the large picture of the Bible narrative or the overview of an Old Testament prophet or one of Paul's letters. On its own, this approach is a supplement, but not a balanced diet.

DAILY READINGS WITH ASSISTANCE

Many Christians use Bible reading notes that are based on a syllabus to ensure that, over time, large parts of the Bible will be covered. Some of these are age-graded so that from the youngest children to adults there is a suitable programme. As an example, one publisher produces a series from age four to adults.[2]

> *Table Talk*, for children aged 4 to 12, is an active and exciting approach for the young family with their parents. It requires only a few minutes, but introduces the good habit of daily Bible reading.
>
> *Explore the Bible (XTB)*, for ages 7 to 11 is packed with things for the youngsters to do on their own as they travel through the Bible. Puzzles, pictures and prayers. *XTB* has full-colour illustrations and is a series of twelve books which, if used on a quarterly basis, will help a child cover all of the main books, themes and characters of the Bible in three years.
>
> *Discover*, for young teens ages 11 to 13 encourages them to get serious with the Bible. '*Discover* takes the reader through the Bible in action-packed, hard-hitting daily chunks. It delivers God's truth straight and in a no-nonsense way—and it's fun—with puzzles, prayer and pondering sections.' Major Bible books, events and characters are covered over a three-year period.
>
> *Engage*, for 14 years and upwards helps young people to dig into the Bible, discovering who God is and what he is like; seeing what God has done through Jesus; and exploring practical ways of living for him.

---

1 Day One Publications offer a series of 365 days of Bible readings with commentaries from C H Spurgeon, John Newton, William Wilberforce, J C Ryle, John Calvin and others. The Good Book Company have, for example, *For the Love of God* by Don Carson.

2 A series from The Good Book Company (Epsom, Surrey, UK).

There are also topical features in each edition on relevant issues such as drugs, alcohol, self-esteem, authority of the Bible, the Holy Spirit and death.

Explore, for adults is more in-depth and covers a much wider area of the Bible. Each daily *Explore* study uses questions and explanatory comments to get the reader digging into the passage.

TRAVELLING THROUGH COMPLETE BOOKS WITH A COMMENTARY

To go deeper and follow a more challenging Bible study approach, there are many excellent commentaries graded from a simple series to the more in-depth commentaries on particular books.[3] The best advice for the initial or average reader is not to be too ambitious. A two or three volume study on Isaiah or Romans for example, will demand a great deal of self-discipline, mental stamina—and time. For those who have all of these, such an in-depth study will prove rewarding, but for those who are simply over-ambitious, it will be discouraging. It is far better to begin with a commentary that enables a whole book to be completed within a few weeks at most.[4] This approach is necessarily slow; it would take many years, if not a lifetime, to cover the whole Bible. This means that there will be large areas of Scripture that are never read, apart from what may be covered in public worship.

READING THE WHOLE BIBLE

By far the best way to read the Bible is from the beginning to the end—all of it. In the eighteenth century John Newton wrote to a lady:

'I know not a better rule of reading the Scripture, than to read it through from beginning to end; and when we have finished it once, to begin it again. We shall meet with many passages which we can make little improvement [value] of, but not so many in the second reading as in the first, and fewer in the third than in the second:

3 Most of the reliable evangelical publishers in the UK, like Day One, The Good Book Company, Evangelical Press and Christian Focus have their graded series. They will be happy to advise an appropriate level.

4 The Day One Publications 'Opening up' series generally meets this criterion.

providing we pray to Him who has the keys to open our understanding, and to anoint our eyes with His spiritual ointment…'[5]

The nineteenth century evangelical preacher Charles Haddon Spurgeon read his entire Bible four times every year—but he was exceptional.

One of the weaknesses of Christians today is that we don't know how the books of the Bible fit together, or what its great themes are, or where Jesus can be found throughout the Scriptures. We are no longer familiar with the biblical narratives of Abraham, Isaac, Jacob, Joseph and Moses, and beyond into Joshua, Saul, David, Solomon and the forty kings of Israel and Judah, then the prophets and the great empires that periodically enslaved Israel—and much more. Through these accounts we will learn about God and his character and purposes.

It is exciting to set out on the adventure of reading the Bible all through, and to read it chronologically to learn how everything fits together. There are many reading programs that will assist us in this. Chapter 7 in this book provides a reading programme to enable the reader to cover—in around eighteen months—the whole Old and New Testaments once and much of the New Testament twice. Chapters 4 and 6 outline the chronological order of the Old and New Testaments showing how the prophets and the letters of the apostles fit into the narrative.

Before setting out to read the whole Bible, Book 1 in this series would prove a helpful introduction. Not only is it designed to introduce the overall theme of the Bible and some of the more remarkable prophecies, but it will confirm the Bible as an authentic book, with much of it revealing the evidence of eyewitnesses. Book 1 will encourage the reader to look out for many interesting details as they travel through the millennia of biblical history.

We should read the Bible prayerfully

This does not simply mean beginning with the prayer: 'Open my eyes that I may see wonderful things in your law' (Psalm 119:18), but reading in

5 *The Works of the Reverend John Newton* (Henry G Bohn and Simpkin Marshall and Co., London 1871), p. 1030, 'Miscellaneous Papers Extracted from Periodical Publications': 'On reading the Bible'.

an attitude of dependence upon God. Acknowledging that whilst there is much in the Bible that is plain even for a young child to understand—and that is the privilege of the Bible, we can teach it to our youngest children—there are also things that are hard to understand, or when understood, are even harder to accept. There are parts that, left to ourselves, we may misunderstand or miss completely. There are also parts that we may twist tortuously to make the Bible say what we want it to say, rather than what God intends it to say. When we come to the Bible we want a godly mind that thinks like God would have us think. Or, as the apostle Paul expressed it: 'We have the mind of Christ' (1 Corinthians 2:16).

We should read the Bible expectantly

The psalmist expected what he called 'wonderful things' to be revealed to his mind from God's word. Those who have been reading the Bible for many years will readily admit that they are still discovering new things. Not novel things, but things that have always been there; things that were never seen before or had been long forgotten. It is always thrilling to see how the books of the Bible add to the developing plan of God's salvation and how people and events fit the great themes of God. It is especially encouraging to see how the promises of the coming Messiah are at first less clear but become clearer as the Old Testament progresses.

After his resurrection, Jesus fell in step with two disciples who were travelling home from Jerusalem to their village of Emmaus. They did not recognize him, but as they travelled on together: 'Beginning with Moses and all the Prophets, he explained to them what was said in all the Scriptures concerning himself.' The fact that this was the most thrilling Bible study they had ever heard is evident by what they said immediately after he left them: 'Were not our hearts burning within us while he talked with us on the road and opened the Scriptures to us?' (Luke 24:32).

They were Jews and had heard those Scriptures read many times before in their synagogue, but they had never put them together until now. Those Old Testament Scriptures that Jesus was quoting, were referring to himself, the longed-for Messiah. Suddenly, it all made sense. These two disciples were seeing 'wonderful things'.

We should never read the Bible regularly in order to be a 'good Christian'. It is to be enjoyed, not endured. There are some parts that are hard to understand, and others that are repetitious; there are mysteries that leave us puzzled. But there is so much that is to be dug from this gold mine and enjoyed.

To see Jesus again and again in the Bible.

To hear God's challenge, correcting, rebuking, training, moulding us more into the likeness of Jesus.

To learn how to counsel ourselves from the Bible in times of discouragement and fear and failure.

To be thrilled by what God is saying.

The books of the cults and world religions, as well as the inscriptions of the religions of the Ancient Near East, have no unfolding record of God's plan over the entire span of human history since creation. They have no beautiful weave like the Christian Bible, as book after book fits together like a divine tapestry nudging the reader closer and closer to the time when 'God sent his Son, born of a woman, born under law, to redeem those under law, that we might receive the full rights of sons.' (Galatians 4:4–5). It is thrilling to watch the progress of God's plan from creation, through prophecy and narrative, until the coming of Christ and the birth and growth of his church

Here is how one of our modern hymn writers, expresses the rich heritage that is ours in the Bible:

Powerful in making us wise to salvation,
witness to faith in Christ Jesus the Word;
breathed out for all by the life-giving Father—
these are the Scriptures, and thus speaks the Lord.

2. Hammer for action and compass for travel,
map in the desert and lamp in the dark;
teaching, rebuking, correcting and training—
these are the Scriptures, and this is their work.

3. History, prophecy, song and commandment,
gospel and letter and dream from on high;
words of the wise who were steered by the Spirit—
these are the Scriptures; on them we rely.

4. Gift for God's servants to fit them completely,
fully equipping to walk in his ways;
guide to good work and effective believing—
these are the Scriptures, for these we give praise!

Christopher Idle (*Praise!* 551) © Author/Jubilate Hymns.

We must read the Bible obediently

In Psalm 119:20 the psalmist writes, 'my soul is consumed with longing for your laws at all times.' That is not a man who wants simply to enjoy the Bible 'stories' or absorb a little bit of theology. It is a man who wants the word of God to take control of him, guide him and direct him day by day.

He wants God's word to hedge him in so that he will not stray from the path of righteousness, to control his conscience so that he will be touch-sensitive to sin. He wants to counsel himself from God's word. Using it to encourage and lift him up when he is downcast; then point him in the right direction through the moral maze of his contemporary society.

The psalmist obeyed it passionately. The phrase in v. 32 'set my heart free' is literally, 'enlarge my heart' in the sense of well-being and joy. That is exactly what Paul meant when he wrote:

'As for you, continue in what you have learned and have become convinced of, because you know those from whom you learned it, and how from infancy you have known the holy Scriptures, which are able to make you wise for salvation through faith in Christ Jesus. All Scripture is God-breathed and is useful for teaching, rebuking, correcting and training in righteousness, so that the man of God may be thoroughly equipped for every good work.' (2 Timothy 3:14–16).

2. Reading the Bible with common sense

The Bible is a treasure chest, full of great value. But it requires a key to unlock it. That key is within the reach of everyone and not just a special group of people with expert training.

This key to understand the principles of interpreting the Bible is called 'hermeneutics', from a Greek word meaning 'interpreter'. The Bible, like any other book, must be understood according to certain rules, and most of these rules we use every day when we read books, newspapers, letters, or emails. When a friend tells us that she 'cried all night', or the radio claims that 'the whole town was angry', we are not expected to believe that our friend sobbed without interruption for eight hours, or that there was not even one person in the town who was not pleased with the news that annoyed most of the citizens. We have used the key of hermeneutics to unlock the statements made.

The Bible as a book must be interpreted sensibly, and as God's book it must be interpreted spiritually. Many of the attacks made upon the Bible by its critics are due to a misunderstanding of proper interpretation. A simple example is when people criticize the Bible for being unscientific when it refers to the sun rising and setting (for example in Genesis 15:12,17; 19:23). This is a convenient expression that is used the world over; it is not intended as a scientific description of the relationship of the sun to the earth. Even meteorologists refers to 'sunset' and 'sunrise'.

The higher our claim for the Bible, the more careful we must be to understand it correctly. We rightly complain about the critic who denies the truth of the Bible and therefore destroys its message, but it is possible to do exactly the same by breaking all the rules of interpretation and making the Bible say what it was never intended to say. When society changes its values, or Christians find themselves living in a different culture, there is a great danger in allowing these changes or that culture to influence the way we understand the Bible. We make the Bible fit into a world view rather than God's view. This happens when we re-interpret the plain text of Scripture to fit with the current theories of science and the fashionable conclusions of morality.

Don Carson expresses his concern in this way: 'Some of us, who would never dream of formally disentangling some parts of the Bible from the rest and declaring them less authoritative than other parts, can by exegetical ingenuity get the Scriptures to say just about whatever we want—and this we thunder to the age as if it were a prophetic word, when it is little more than the message of the age bounced off Holy Scripture.'[6] The prophet Jeremiah complained about the same thing: 'How can you say, "We are wise, for we have the law of the Lord", when actually the lying pen of the scribes has handled it falsely?' (Jeremiah 8:8).

The interpretation of Scripture is a vital subject; it is as important as the doctrine of inerrancy itself. There is no value in claiming, 'These are the words of God,' if we then proceed to interpret them in a way directly opposite to God's intention. Hermeneutics is not a matter of theory; it always has a practical application. The preacher and Bible teacher cannot explain or apply the Scripture unless there are clear principles for interpreting it.

Much of the Bible is plain, and anyone with a little common sense can understand it; however, some of it is hard to grasp, and at times there is a fuller or deeper meaning that is not immediately obvious. See in this series Book 2 chapter 4 under 'A fuller meaning' for more on this. Both the prophet Isaiah and Jesus himself reminded us that it is one thing to hear the word of God, but quite another to understand it (Isaiah 6:9–10; Matthew 13:13–15). An Amish bishop is on record as saying, 'There are no mysteries in the Bible. God never made no mysteries. But, brethren, there are some tight points.' Hermeneutics helps us not only in the plain areas, to keep them plain, but also in those 'tight points', so that we shall not compound difficulties with our own foolishness.

---

6 *Hermeneutics, Authority and Canon*, ed. D A Carson and John D Woodbridge (Inter-Varity Press, Leicester, UK, 1986), p. 47, 'Recent Developments in the Doctrine of Scripture'.

What follows in this chapter and the next is only an introduction to the much wider issue of understanding the Bible.[7] We will set out several basic questions that we should ask whenever we want to understand a passage, or even a single verse, of the Bible.

What kind of passage is this?

The word that is used to explain a type of literature is known as the 'genre' of the passage. By genre, is meant the category or style of writing intended by the original writer and how he would expect it to be understood by the readers. We must be careful not to superimpose how we think a passage should be understood before grasping what the original writer intended and how the original readers would have read it.

IS IT HISTORY?

If a passage of Scripture is clearly historical then we must remember that its purpose is to describe things that actually happened. Generally, it is not difficult to know which passages are historical and which are not. For example, it could hardly be denied that the records of the various kings of Israel and Judah are expected to be taken as actual accounts of their lives; if anyone wants to deny this, the responsibility is theirs to prove that they are not intended as true accounts. On the other hand, it is equally clear that the 'event' told by Jotham in Judges 9:8–15 is in picture language; it would be a foolish person who criticized the Bible, or Jotham, for thinking that the trees actually held a conversation.

We should always decide on the answer to this first question before we go any further. For example, when the reader turns to the opening chapters of Genesis, the book of Jonah, or the miracles of Jesus, the first question must not be: 'How can I understand this in the light of current scientific thinking?' but, 'Is this written as history?' We cannot pick and choose to suit our convenience. If those three examples are poetry or 'myth' then how can we ever know what is historical truth? We may choose not

7 This is an important but at times, complex subject. For a more comprehensive study of the subject, the reader will benefit from Gordon D Fee and Douglas Stuart, *How to Read the Bible for All Its Worth* (Zondervan, originally 1982, fourth edition 2014).

to believe their accuracy, but if we follow the rules of hermeneutics we cannot seriously doubt the intention that these are to be accepted as fact.

We should never start with the 'problems' a passage presents, but first of all be clear what type of passage it is. The miraculous conception of the child in the womb of the virgin Mary, ensuring that Jesus was both fully God and fully man, can never be explained in scientific terms. Our first question to answer is, 'Are these accounts written and intended as statements of historical fact—that they really happened this way?'

IS IT POETRY?

Some passages of the Bible are poetic and we will not therefore look for detailed accuracy in matters of fact. If we turn to Psalm 104, Job 38, or Isaiah 40:12–15, for example, we have what are clearly poetic descriptions of creation. The words and phrases are very different from Genesis and no one could seriously suggest that the Bible views God as riding on the clouds like a man in a chariot (Psalm 104:3), or stopping the oceans with immense doors (Job 38:8), or weighing the mountains in a gigantic pair of scales (Isaiah 40:12). This language is poetic and nothing like it is found in the historical Genesis account.

In the sixteenth century, when Galileo discovered that the earth revolved around the sun, he was contradicted by church leaders on the basis that Psalm 93:1 (see also 96:10; 104:5) claimed, 'The world is firmly established, it will not be moved.' This was a sad ignorance of the fact that these passages are written in poetic style (genre) and are intended only to imply the fixed certainty of God's plans and laws both for man and his creation. Did the church authorities of his day really believe that God sits on a throne and that the oceans have a voice (vv. 2–3)? We must always be ready to recognize poetry in the Bible.

IS IT PROPHECY?

Understanding prophecy is perhaps the most difficult (and contentious) part of Bible hermeneutics. Once we recognise that a passage is prophetic we will be looking out for certain things. Prophecy is not merely telling the future (fore-telling) but telling God's word for the day in which the prophet lived (forth-telling). Poetry played a large part in the language of the prophets and we are wise not to take all their words as having a literal fulfilment. We shall return to this later, but there is another significant question to answer whenever we come to a passage of prophecy, and that is the matter of timing: when will this prophecy be fulfilled? There are at least six possibilities in answering this question.

- Is the prophet referring only to something God is going to carry out in the prophet's own day?
- Is he referring to what God will do later on in the Old Testament, beyond the prophet's own day. Some of Isaiah's prophecies, for example, look forward to the return from exile under Cyrus, over a century and a half later.
- Is the prophet referring to what will happen when the Messiah comes and brings in the 'gospel age' after the death and resurrection of Jesus? This is clearly the case in Jeremiah 31:31–33 for example.
- Those who believe in a millennial end-time experience when, for a thousand years, Jesus will reign in Jerusalem over a willingly submissive people, may understand some prophecies referring to this period. This is a pre-millennial view.
- Or it may refer to the golden age of gospel success just before the return of Jesus in glory. That is a post-millennial view.
- Or the passage may refer to the promise of the ultimate new heaven and new earth. An a-millennial view.

Isaiah 11 and 35 are two passages that can be understood in each of the last three ways, depending upon the view of end-time fulfilment of prophecy. This is a difficult matter, but there is no alternative to working hard at the passage if we are to understand what God is saying to us today.

Closely connected with the prophetic language of Isaiah or Ezekiel in the Old Testament is the language of John's Revelation in the New Testament. This also is a form of prophecy that is referred to as 'apocalyptic' language. We will consider this in the next chapter.

A few simple rules will help us when faced with prophecy in Scripture.

- What is the context? Who was the prophet? To whom was he speaking? What was happening in the world around him at the time?
- What was the relevance of the prophecy to the prophet's own day? We should always ask this question before we run ahead to see if there is something for our own day as well.
- Is there a Messianic fulfilment, as in Isaiah 9:2–7, 53:1–12 and Micah 5:2? Sometimes there is both an immediate and a future fulfilment. Many prophecies in the Old Testament point on to the coming of the Messiah, but this is not true of them all and we do not have to find the Messiah where he is not.
- Is the prophecy, which points to a future fulfilment, conditional? Micah warned Jerusalem of a judgement that would come if the city did not turn back to God (Jeremiah 26:17–19); in the time of Hezekiah the people did repent and the judgement of God did not fall. Similarly, Jonah's warnings to Nineveh were tempered by the offer of mercy if the inhabitants repented. Many of the promises given to Israel were conditional upon their obedience to him.
- Is the language that of poetry or is it to be taken literally? This is often one of the hardest questions to answer and we must interpret carefully. Isaiah's picture in chapter 11 of the wolf and lamb, leopard and kid, lion and calf and the young child, clearly was not fulfilled in Isaiah's own day, but does it refer symbolically to the benefits of Christ's gospel or literally to the new heavens and new earth at the end of time? It will be helpful to remember that even when an Old Testament prophecy is looking forward to the time of the Messiah, or further into the final age of the new heavens and new earth, it will be using language that would be familiar to the prophet's own day. Therefore, the pictures in the book of Revelation are of the best that we know here—gold, silver, precious stones and crystal—but we may suspect there are even better things in the reality of the new world.

- The most important principle of all is the way in which an Old Testament prophecy is used in the New Testament. This is so important that a few examples will be useful.

The passage in Isaiah 9:2–7 is a prophecy, seven hundred years before the event, of the coming Messiah. From the words in verse 7 we might have expected the Messiah literally to revive the monarchy in Israel and reign as king in Jerusalem; this is exactly how many Jews understood it. However, because we can look back at the actual fulfilment of Isaiah 9:7 (compare Luke 1:67–79), we conclude that those words have a spiritual fulfilment and not a literal, historical, fulfilment. This is a warning to be careful when we expect a literal fulfilment of other prophecies of the future. Sometimes we are right to expect a literal fulfilment, but not always.

Another example is found in Joel 2. Our understanding of this chapter is governed by its fulfilment in Acts 2. According to Peter, Joel 2:28–32 is a prophecy of the gift of the Holy Spirit at Pentecost (compare Acts 2:14–21). This being so, the situation described in Joel 2:1–27 must be a picture of Jesus' earthly ministry, because verse 28 says, 'And afterwards…' and then follows the description Peter quoted at Pentecost. For the same reason, the prophecy of Joel 3 must begin to be fulfilled at Pentecost, because Joel 3:1 promises, 'In those days and at that time…' Since we are taught by the New Testament to understand Joel 2 in a spiritual way—referring to Christ and his church—it is only consistent hermeneutics that we also interpret chapter 3 spiritually as referring to the church and the gospel age up to the Day of Judgement.

In Amos 9:11–12 there are references to God repairing and rebuilding 'David's fallen tent' so that it may possess the 'remnant of Edom and all the nations that bear my name'. What does that mean? In Acts 15:16–17 James leaves us in no doubt: he told the Council at Jerusalem that it was fulfilled when the gospel was given to the Gentiles.

Whilst many prophecies in the Old Testament point on to the coming of the Messiah, this is not true of them all. When the prophet Jeremiah promised a return of Israel from the land of exile after seventy years (Jeremiah 25:11,12 and 29:11–14), it was a promise accurately fulfilled after the triumph of Persia over Babylonia in 539 BC. However, even here there is a timeless promise that Christians have rightly taken from the God who always has good plans for his chosen people in every age.

These brief illustrations should help us in our interpretation of many other Old Testament prophetic passages. Remember, the New Testament must be our guide, and our understanding must be consistent with the whole Bible.

What is the context?

One of the greatest dangers when using the Bible is to take a verse, phrase or passage out of its place within the Bible—we call this the context. No text is ever improved from being taken out of its context. Every word of the Bible has three contexts. We may think of these as the room, the house, and the street in which the word lives.

THE ROOM—THE BIBLICAL CONTEXT

It is important always to read a verse and the passage around it. We should not be influenced too much by the chapter and verse divisions of the Bible. They are not part of the God-breathed Scripture. See Book 4 chapter 2 in this series under 'Where did the chapters and verses come from?'

Several questions must be asked in this room: 'To whom is the writer speaking? Israel or the nations? Christians or non-Christians? Young or old? Obedient or disobedient?' For example, the familiar verse used to encourage the unbeliever to 'open the door of his heart and let Jesus in' is found in Revelation 3:20: 'Here I am! I stand at the door and knock. If anyone hears my voice and opens the door, I will come in and eat with him, and he with me.' But the context leaves us in no doubt that it is a backsliding Christian church that is being addressed here, not the unbeliever.

We must also ask, 'Do the verses around help to explain this one?' If we take a phrase out of its context, Joshua 24:15 provides a perfect challenge for the close of an evangelistic service: 'Choose for yourselves this day whom you will serve.' The application could be, 'The choice is yours, Christ or the world.' However, that is not what Joshua was saying.

He was speaking to those who had already rejected the Lord, and his challenge was this: 'Go home and choose which one of the idols of the other nations you will follow.' With a little thought, this verse is still an excellent evangelistic text, but not in the way it is normally used. A verse should always be read in its biblical context—the verses and chapters around it.

THE HOUSE—THE HISTORICAL CONTEXT

When reading a passage of the Bible, the question must always be asked, 'What was happening in the world around Judaea at this time?' The Bible is a book full of history, and that means that every book and every passage has a historical context. Many of the prophecies of Isaiah or Jeremiah make little sense if the reader is not aware of the threats being made by Assyria, Syria or Babylon. Who were these nations and what was their relationship with Israel at the time this book was written? Many of the psalms become more vivid when we know that David wrote them while he was an outlaw in the desert from King Saul, with a price on his head.

Many incidents in the Gospels, Luke 2:1–3 for example, lose much of their meaning if we do not understand that Rome was the governing nation and kept a strong army of occupation in Palestine. The 'second mile' of Matthew 5:41 is a direct reference to the right of the Roman legionary to compel an Israelite to carry his pack for one Roman mile. The answer to this historical question is often found in the Bible itself, so we do not require a great knowledge of ancient history, but a good Bible commentary will certainly help.

THE STREET—THE CULTURAL CONTEXT

Anyone who is seriously interested in understanding the Bible will take a keen interest in the culture of Bible times.[8] The writers, whether Old or New Testament, were always writing against the background of the life

8 *The Book of Acts in its First Century Setting* covers the context of the first century in great depth and provides a rich store of information. Ed. Bruce Winter (William B Eerdmans Publishing Company, Grand Rapids MI and The Paternoster Press, Carlisle UK). There are six volumes, but they are valuable for the serious Bible student.

and times in which they lived and, inevitably, this is reflected in their work. Frequently, the radical contrast between that culture and Christian values is in focus. A few examples will illustrate this.

- Marriage was fragile and temporary then as now. The prevalence of dysfunctional families and loose sexual relationships was as familiar to the early Christians as we are today; they too had to contend with broken homes and lives. The strong emphasis by the apostles on the importance of the marriage bond and purity in sexual conduct, reflects the contrast of loose relationships in the pagan world. When Paul wrote that 'the wife's body does not belong to her alone', he immediately balanced it with 'in the same way, the husband's body does not belong to him alone' (1 Corinthians 7:4). The whole context of the physical relationship in marriage is that of equality and purity (Hebrews 13:4). Similarly, the reference of Paul to the wife's 'submission' to her husband (Ephesians 5:22) must never be separated from the context in which he immediately commands husbands to 'love your wives as Christ loved the church and gave himself up for her' (v. 25). This is one of the most beautiful passages found in any literature on the relationship of men and women in the marriage bond and, not incidentally, provides a basis for the true Christian definition of marriage. Peter follows the same approach in 1 Peter 3:1–7. Similarly, Elders must have only one wife (1 Timothy 3:2); no Christian should prostitute their body with easy sex (1 Corinthians 6:15–20); young men should learn self-control (Titus 2:6); and 'sexual immorality, impurity and debauchery' are contrasted with the fruit of the Spirit, 'love, joy, peace, patience, kindness, goodness, faithfulness, gentleness and self-control' (Galatians 5:19, 22–23). All this was radical.
- Although both Old and New Testaments are set against the background of a patriarchal society in which men were in charge, in the first century Roman and Greek culture, some women were wealthy and ran their own business. Lydia, in the expensive designer trade, is an example (Acts 16). Some women were patrons of a pagan temple. Acts 13:50 and 17:4 and 12 refer to 'prominent' women in society; the two words

used refer to those who are leading women of high standing (ESV).[9] Therefore, the suggestion that Paul and Peter followed a supposed pattern of total male dominance should be treated with caution.

- To understand the widespread system of slavery throughout the Roman empire will help to appreciate that the New Testament was far from acquiescent in the practice. In 1 Timothy 1:10 Paul wrote against 'slave-traders' (ESV 'enslavers') in the context of 'adulterers and perverts ... liars and perjurers', and reminded masters that they were answerable to God for the way they treat their servants (Ephesians 6:9). He also changed the whole relationship between a Christian employer and his servants (1 Timothy 6:2 and Philemon). James reserved his strongest condemnation for the wealthy who oppress the poor (James 5:1–6).
- Much of the Bible involved people who lived in sheep-rearing or fishing communities and it may be hard for a businessman in a modern city to understand this way of life. Passages like Psalm 23 and John 10:1–16 become more meaningful when we understand the foolish and helpless nature of sheep and the caring of a good shepherd. Jesus' parables about separating sheep from goats, or wheat from tares, take on a greater significance when we appreciate how similar in appearance are eastern sheep and goats, and how hard it can be to distinguish wild oats from the real crop.
- Almost invariably, the images of the emperors and the gods were depicted as manly and handsome because the Greeks and Romans believed that physical beauty was equated with moral virtue. Beautiful and good was the pinnacle of true humanity. This was expressed by the phrase: *kalos kai agathos*—beautiful and virtuous. The greatest virtue for both Greeks and Romans was to be sufficiently wealthy, healthy, educated and aristocratic that there was no need to work. Slaves and other labourers were therefore locked out of the possibility of being beautiful and virtuous. It is immediately obvious how different were the Christian values. Constantly in the teaching of Jesus and the apostles, the

9 See above, volume 2, the 'Graeco-Roman setting'. pp. 114–117.

fragility and futility of grasping for more is exposed (eg Matthew 16:26; 1 Timothy 6:17; Hebrews 10:34; 13:5; James 4:1–3; 5:1–6; Revelation 3:17), and the importance of honest and hard work is honoured (Acts 18:3; 1 Corinthians 4:12; Ephesians 4:28; 2 Thessalonians 3:10–12).

- Similarly, in Roman culture, those who saw the emperor's image on a coin or inscription were expected to understand that it was as though the emperor himself was in front of them. Paul used this familiar concept to describe the Lord Jesus as the 'image of the invisible God' (Colossians 1:15). He meant that when we 'see' Jesus (meet with him by faith), we see God (2 Corinthians 4:4–6).
- A little knowledge of the seven cities referred to in Revelation 2–3 will make the message to the church in each city much more vivid. For example, Laodicea (Revelation 3:14–22) piped its water into the city from distant hot springs and it therefore arrived lukewarm (v. 16); it was also a wealthy banking city (v. 17), and boasted an eye hospital producing a special eye ointment (vv. 17–18).
- Even more important, such knowledge of local conditions can avoid misunderstandings. Matthew 16:19 has been frequently misunderstood and wrongly applied in the history of the Christian church. The Jewish custom of presenting a scribe with a key as a symbol of his office in interpreting the law, helps to understand the whole passage correctly.
- 2 Samuel 19:8 reads that, 'The king got up and took his seat in the gateway. When the men were told, "The king is sitting in the gateway," they all came before him.' This carries more meaning when we are aware that the gate of the city was like the town hall of today: it was the place where the leaders met to carry out their civic and political functions. Incidentally, this may well indicate that in the book of Esther Mordecai was not 'sitting at the king's gate' because he was out of work, on the contrary, it may imply that he was occupying an important position in government (Esther 2:19).[10]

10 For an intriguing possibility that the biblical Mordecai has been identified see *Evidence for the Bible* (Day One Publications, Leominster, UK, 2014), p. 101.

The context of every Bible verse is the biblical room, the historical house and the street of local customs. The first is essential; the other two are very helpful. But even if we do not have access to books that will help to understand the house and the street, we will still be able to understand God's word and benefit from it providing we stay in the biblical room.

What is the plain meaning?

After we have asked, 'What kind of passage is this?' and 'What is the context?' our next question is 'What is the plain meaning of this passage?' This is an obvious question, but readers can be so busy looking for problems or hidden meanings that they forget to ask it. Sometimes the question is put in a different way: 'What is the grammatical sense? What do the words mean?'. To answer this question, it is essential that we have an accurate translation in front of us and not a paraphrase. See Book 4 chapter 5 in this series. No translation is completely free from some paraphrasing, but hermeneutics is concerned with accuracy. If we do not know Hebrew (the language of the Old Testament) or Greek (the language of the New Testament), we will have to trust that the translators have given an accurate version of the words and grammar into our own language.

Every language has its own rules of grammar and we must interpret the Bible according to those rules. For example, many young Christians find difficulty in 1 John 3:9 because it may appear from some translations that to commit one sin disqualifies them from being a Christian. However, the Greek verb used is what is called a 'present continuous' tense and it would be correct, in this context, to paraphrase it: 'No one born of God goes on and on committing sin as a way of life.' The *English Standard Version* brings out the meaning of the verb with: 'No one born of God makes a practice of sinning.'

Does, 'Do not move around from house to house' (Luke 10:7) forbid door-to-door evangelism? Or does, 'The highest heavens belong to the LORD, but the earth he has given to man' (Psalm 115:16) forbid space exploration? Is 'If someone strikes you on the right cheek, turn to him the other also' (Matthew 5:39) really an invitation to the mugger to 'do us over' a second time? Context and common sense should provide us with an answer. The Bible is intended to be relevant, not ridiculous. This leads us to ask a further question.

What do the words actually mean?

Occasional problems arise in understanding a passage because we do not really know what a particular word means. However, there are many pitfalls in this, and in what follows we can only hint at some of them.[11] There are several questions we can ask about the words used in a passage.

WHAT IS THE NORMAL MEANING OF THE WORD AND HOW IS IT USED ELSEWHERE IN THE BIBLE?

A good Bible concordance is essential for this. Sometimes knowing the normal meaning of words can make our understanding of a passage more valuable. Much has been made of John 21 where Jesus asked Peter three times if he loved him. Peter was eager to express his love, and in verse 17 replied, 'Lord, you know all things; you know that I love you.' In the Greek Peter used two different words for 'know'. The first meant, 'You know everything perfectly (intuitively) because of who you are,' while the second meant, 'You know by experience that I love you.' In addition, Jesus used the verb *agapaō* (love) in vv. 15 and 16, and three times Peter responded with a different word for love (*philō*). When Jesus asked Peter the third time 'do you love me' (v. 17) he picked up Peter's verb *philō*.

However, there are important cautions to be aware of: First, sometimes a word is used simply for variety without any deeper significance; every writer knows the importance of not repeating the same word in a sentence unless it is for special emphasis. Although there are no true synonyms in Greek any more than in English, some words with slight variations may be used simply for variety. The response of Peter referred to above may come in this category. The two verbs for love, *agapaō* and *philō*, each have

11 See D A Carson, *Exegetical Fallacies*, 2nd ed. (Baker Books. Grand Rapids. MI. 1999). Every Bible preacher/teacher would be wise to read this book (twice). It is a straightforward yet scholarly introduction to a complex subject. The warnings are essential for any Bible teacher. However, the use of a helpful book like this should not be allowed to make us despair of ever being sure of the meaning of a word.

a different nuance, but they are also used interchangeably and it is unwise to make much of the use of one against the other. For example, *agapaō* is used for Demas' love of the world (2 Timothy 4:10) and for the Father's love of his Son (John 15:9)—and in 5:20 *philō* is used of the love of the Father for the Son![12]

In this same context, is there necessarily a significance in Jesus' reference to 'sheep' twice and 'lambs' once? We might suggest that he refers to Peter's future ministry among mature and immature Christians—or adults and children—but this cannot be certain. Jesus may simply be using variety.

A second caution is that the same word can have a variety of meanings, depending upon its context; simply looking up a word in the dictionary will not always help.

The key is that a word has the meaning intended by its use. Consider the following statements:

'I am very *positive* about his future role in this company'
'I am *positive* that what I am telling you is correct'
'That habit is *positively* disgusting'
'In the electrical plug, the brown lead is the *positive* one'
'His answer to the problem was very *positive*'
'He has a *positive* attitude to those in need'
'*Positive* discrimination is discouraged in this company'

Even a small dictionary will provide at least seven meanings of the word, but to use the word 'certain' in each of these sentences will hardly make sense. The following words will fit each sentence in order: hopeful, certain, downright, live, constructive, helpful, selective—and there are many more uses.

Therefore, the 'normal' meaning of a word may change from one writer to another. Paul frequently uses the word 'called' specifically to refer to those who are chosen by God for salvation (for example Romans 1:6; 8:30; 9:24), whereas in Matthew 22:14 'Many are called, but few are chosen' (*English Standard Version*) the word refers more to an open invitation.

---

12 See above for an extended discussion of these two words, pp. 30 and 51–53.

Used in Romans 3:24 the word *dōrean* means 'freely' and describes the Christian doctrine of justification by the grace of God which is without cost to the recipient. However, exactly the same word is used in John 15:25 where it is translated "They hated me *without reason*' or 'without a cause'. In Galatians 2:21 the same word cannot be translated in either of the above ways but is properly rendered 'if righteousness could be gained through the law, Christ died *for nothing*.' Freely, without reason, for nothing—each is an adequate translation of the same word.

Words may change their meaning over time. The word *martus* referred to someone who bore witness to, or confirmed, an event or a legal document; only subsequently was it invested with the more noble role of dying for the faith.[13] The reference to Stephen in Acts 22:20 is better translated 'witness' (as ESV). The inconsistency of the NIV is seen in its translation of the word *martus* by 'martyr' in Acts 22:20 but 'witness' in Revelation 2:13—in fact both Stephen and Antipas were put to death.

Occasionally the next six questions have to be asked in order to find the answer to this first one.

HOW ARE THE WORDS USED IN THIS PASSAGE?

Sometimes a word is used with a different emphasis according to the purpose of the speaker or writer—as we have seen with the word 'positive' above. An example of this is found in Jesus' words in Luke 14:26: 'If anyone comes to me, and does not hate his father and mother, his wife and children, his brothers and sisters—yes, and even his own life—he cannot be my disciple.' The word normally carries the idea of detesting a thing, but it can also mean to disregard or overlook something in preference to something else. The same word is used in Luke 16:13, where Jesus taught that a man cannot have two masters, not because he will have to hate or detest one, but because, in a conflict of commands, he will have to disregard or overlook one. Therefore, the word 'hate' has a different emphasis here from that which we would normally give it.

---

13 According to J B Lightfoot it is likely that Clement of Rome, before the close of the first century, was the first to use the words martyr and martyrdom with specific reference to those who died for their faith: *Clement of Rome* I: v-vi.

HOW ARE THE WORDS USED ELSEWHERE BY THE SAME WRITER?

We have already illustrated this by the example quoted above from Luke 16:13. The obvious use of the word 'hate' here, helps us to understand the same word in Luke 14:26; at times obedience to God will run contrary to our desire to please our family.

In the Old Testament, an example is found in Isaiah 9:6. Those who deny that Christ really is God insist that this verse claims the Messiah to be 'a mighty god' and that it has no reference to 'Jehovah God'. But in the next chapter (Isaiah 10:21) exactly the same Hebrew phrase, *El Gibbor*, is used—and here the context shows that it can only refer to 'Jehovah God'. It is faulty hermeneutics to assume that Isaiah has changed the meaning of a phrase from one chapter to the next. Besides, this exact phrase, *El Gibbor*, is used nowhere else in the Old Testament and therefore we can only obtain its true application from Isaiah himself—and his use in Isaiah 10:21 leaves us in no doubt.

HOW ARE THE WORDS USED OUTSIDE THE BIBLE?

It is not possible for most of us to do our own research here, but commentaries may help us. Sometimes a word occurs so rarely in the Bible that it is not easy to determine its exact meaning, and an exact meaning may be very important. In Philippians 2:6–7 the word 'nature' or 'form' occurs. The only other place this particular word will be found in the New Testament is in Mark 16:12. Those who deny that Christ was really God claim that the word 'form' in Philippians 2:6 means only that Christ was similar to God or like God, but that he was not really God. The use of this word among pagan writers, shows that the word carries the meaning of 'the nature or essence of a thing'. So we can properly understand Philippians 2:6–7 to mean that Christ always had the true and essential nature of God and that he took upon himself the true and essential nature of a servant.

The Greek word *harpagmon* that is translated in Philippians 2:6 'grasped' is used only here in the Scriptures, but is found frequently outside the Bible. This enabled scholars to fix its meaning as something seized or grasped for one's own advantage. Similarly, in 2 Timothy 3:16, the true meaning of the word *theopneustos* as 'God-breathed' was understood by the use of the word outside the Bible. See in this series Book 2 chapter 2 under 'The meaning of inspiration'.

WHAT DOES THE REST OF THE BIBLE SAY ABOUT THIS SUBJECT?

In Book 5 chapter 4 in this series, under 'Progressive revelation', attention was drawn to the importance of appreciating that God did not provide at once all that he had to say to the human race. As the biblical history progresses, so God reveals more and more of his purposes; no one book of the Bible is wholly sufficient without the others. For this reason, the best commentary upon the Bible is the Bible itself. The New Testament is God's own commentary upon the Old. The New Testament is therefore our infallible commentary upon the Old Testament. We may be unsure how far we can take as statements of truth the words of an unspiritual man, such as Eliphaz, one of Job's critics. In Job 42:7 God condemned the general criticism and argument of Eliphaz, but in 1 Corinthians 3:19 Paul quoted one of his sayings, found in Job 5:13, with approval. That is our authority for saying that where Eliphaz speaks in harmony with the rest of Scripture he may be quoted as speaking the truth, but we dare not take his words as authoritative if they find no support anywhere else in the Bible. The Bible accurately records his words, as it does some of the words of Satan, without giving authority and truth to them.

There are several occasions when the New Testament makes statements and gives information about Old Testament characters or events that are found nowhere in the Old Testament. This is not an error but is God's way of adding to our understanding of what he has already revealed. For example, we learn much about Moses that is not revealed in the Old Testament (see Acts 7:22; Hebrews 11:24–27), including the names of the Egyptian magicians (compare 2 Timothy 3:8 with Exodus 7:11). We also learn facts about Elijah (James 5:17) and Lot (2 Peter 2:7–8) which are not recorded in the Old Testament.

It is easy to condemn Lot for his choice of the fertile valley and his decision to settle in Sodom (Genesis 13); however, Peter refers to him a 'righteous' man who was 'distressed' and 'tormented in his righteous soul by the lawless deeds he saw and heard' in Sodom (2 Peter 2:7–8).

It is essential to discover what else the Bible teaches about the subject contained in a particular verse.

Sometimes the context of the verse cannot help us. The book of Proverbs is a collection of wise sayings and quite often the surrounding verses, or even the chapter, do not say anything to help us on that subject. We must immediately ask, 'Where else does the Bible speak about this?' Always interpret the Bible consistently with itself.

A passage that is difficult to understand must be interpreted in the light of what is clear. Colossians 1:22–23 may seem to teach that our final security and salvation are dependent upon our ability to continue faithfully. But if we turn to John 10:28 and Romans 8:38–39 we can discover how eternally secure the Christian is. In Colossians 1, rather, Paul is challenging the church to see whether or not they really have saving faith in Christ. This is an example of how we have allowed Scripture to govern our interpretation of Scripture.

WHAT DO THE COMMENTARIES SAY?

We are not to be slaves to what other people think, but we should not be indifferent to their conclusions either. A reliable commentary on the Bible is invaluable. There are some excellent modern commentaries today on individual books of the Bible, from the undemanding to those that probe deeper into the text. It is not possible to find a one-volume Bible commentary that will adequately deal with all the verses we need some help with. It is unwise to browse in the local Christian bookshop but far better to take advice from a trusted and more experienced Christian, or keep to trusted Christian publishers. A commentary will not do all the work, but it will steer into the right path and help to avoid errors in understanding the Bible.

Paul's puns

Paul had not only a brilliant mind but he was also a master 'wordsmith'. He enjoyed using words to their best effect to make the greatest impact. Frequently he used puns to fix his teaching in the mind of his readers. A pun is simply a play on words; unfortunately, a pun can rarely be translated into another language. We will not always be aware of this in our translations, but a few examples here show the richness of Paul's letters.

PAUL GIVES NEW MEANING FOR OLD

In Ephesians 2:12 Paul reminded the Ephesians that they were once 'without God in this world'. The word translated 'without God' is *atheos* (atheist). The Christians were accused of being atheists by the Greeks and Romans because they had abandoned the pagan gods. Paul encouraged them to believe the opposite: they were atheists when they trusted the idols.

In Ephesians 4:2 Paul encouraged the young Christians to be 'completely humble'. The word *tapeinos* (humble) was never used in a good sense in the first century; it meant 'low born' or 'small minded' (compare Romans 12:16 'low position'). Paul dresses it in Christian clothes and commends it as the mind-set of the Christian.

The word for 'boast' (*kauchaomai*) is used only by Paul in the New Testament, but he employed it thirty-five times. Its normal use is of negative boasting with a proud intent, but in Romans 5:2 Paul encouraged the Christians to 'boast' of their hope in God. There is an interesting nuance here which is missed by translating it as 'rejoice'.

A word that Paul used at least ten times in Romans 4 is translated 'credited' or 'counted' (vv. 3–6, 9–11, 22–24). The word was taken from the finance office where it meant 'to calculate' and then to pass money into someone's account. It was an excellent word for Paul to use in order to explain the 'imputed' righteousness of Christ that is passed into the account of the Christian.

Twice Paul described his ministry as that of a 'herald' (*kērux*) of the good news (1 Timothy 2:7; 2 Timothy 1:11). It is unfortunate to translate this with 'preacher', because Paul deliberately used a familiar word that referred to the herald of the ancient world. The herald was equivalent to an ambassador and was accorded diplomatic immunity in peace negotiations. His task was to communicate accurately the sovereign's message and he was considered the mouthpiece of the gods. Paul saw the preacher of the gospel in this light.

PAUL PLAYS ON WORDS WITH SIMILAR SOUNDS

There are many occasions where Paul used words that ring in such a way that the earliest Christians would well remember them. Here are just three:

In Romans 12:3 an English translation 'Do not think of yourself more highly than you ought, but rather think of yourself with sober judgment…' loses Paul's rhythm. In that short verse he employs the word 'think' three times and each time it builds on the previous use: *phronein—huperphronein — sophronein.* We may roughly paraphrase: think, super-think, sober-think. The Christians at Rome would easily remember those three words.

Similarly, in 2 Corinthians 11:3 Paul slipped two words together with a similar ring where 'sincere and pure' are *haplōtatos* and *hagnōtatos*.

In Romans 12:13–14 the apostle used the same verb to urge his readers to 'go after, pursue' (*diōkontes*) hospitality and to bless those who 'go after, pursue' (*diōkontas*) you. This subtlety is inevitably lost in most of our translations.

PAUL COINED NEW WORDS?

It is possible that Paul was equally happy to invent new words. The single word (*sunezōopoiēsen*) translated 'made us alive with' in Ephesians 2:5 and Colossians 2:13 is, as yet, found nowhere among pagan writers. How uniquely Christian is that word!

The word Paul used in Colossians 2:15 and 3:9 ('disarmed' and 'taken off') some scholars think Paul coined in this context for his own use.

The phrase 'God-breathed' in 2 Timothy 3:16, correctly translates the word *theopneustos* (see Book 2 chapter 2 in this series). This word has not been found in any Greek literature prior to Paul's use in this passage.[14]

PAUL'S THEOLOGICAL EMPHASIS

On eleven occasions in Ephesians, Paul begins a verb or noun with a small prefix that means 'with' (*sun*). His is reminding the Ephesians of their 'oneness' in Christ since the great barrier between Jew and Gentile has been destroyed (2:14). If we translate that small preposition *sun* by 'together', and hyphenate it, his emphasis will be clear.

---

14 A full discussion of this word will be found in B B Warfield *Inspiration and Authority of the Bible* (The Presbyterian and Reformed Publishing Company, Philadelphia, 1948), pp. 245–296. See p. 248 for the conclusion of its earliest known use by Paul. Even then, not until the mid-second century AD was it regularly used to describe the origin of the Scriptures.

In 2:5–6 three verbs are prefixed with *sun*: we are 'made-alive-together', 'raised-up-together', 'seated-together with Christ'.

In 2:19–22 three more words are prefixed with *sun*: 'citizens-together', 'joined-together', 'built-together'.

In 3:6 three nouns are prefixed with *sun*: 'heirs-together', 'members-together', 'sharers-together'.

In 4:16 two verbs describe the church 'joined-together' and 'held-together'.

Conclusion

We have seen that there are rules for understanding the Bible and that we cannot simply make up our own mind according to what we would like the Bible to say. It is the revelation of God, and it is therefore far too important to be read carelessly.

For most of us who have no knowledge of Hebrew or Greek, we need have little fear in taking up a good translation and reading the most obvious meaning from the text and, if we want to dig deeper, use the aid of a reliable commentary.

Some of what has been written above is of greater relevance to those who have a little knowledge of the original languages. It can be a dangerous delight to present a theological argument based on the etymology of a word, the conjugation of a verb or the syntax of a sentence![15] Dangerous, because such details do not always prove a point. Scholars expend hours of academic time, reams of print-outs, and libraries of books disagreeing on small points of exegesis. The Bible was not written for scholars to tease out subtleties, but for ordinary people to know the mind of God.

When William Tyndale in 1521 (and Desiderius Erasmus before him) determined to make the Bible speak for the ploughboy, he did so with a knowledge of the complexities of etymology, conjugations and syntax, but he knew that a faithful translation would do the hard work for the reader, who could then enjoy and learn from the Bible.

---

15 If you really want to know: etymology is the study of the original meaning of words, conjugation is the form of verbs and syntax is the structure of a sentence. All this is part of grammar.

3. A bit more common sense

Like any other book, the Bible uses forms of speech, and recognizing these forms of speech is essential to a proper understanding of Scripture.

Forms of speech

SIMILE

A simile is a vivid yet simple comparison of one thing with another. Peter uses a simile in 1 Peter 5:8: 'Your enemy the devil prowls around like a roaring lion.' The devil is not literally a lion; he is like a lion in his fierce attack upon believers.

METAPHOR

A metaphor is the description of something using words that do not literally apply to it. In a metaphor, the words 'like' and 'as' are omitted and something is described as if it really was something else. For example, in Luke 13:32 our Lord does not say that Herod is *like* a fox but, to make his description stronger, he uses a metaphor and says that Herod *is* a fox. The reference to the 'floodgates of the heavens' in Genesis 7:11 is a metaphor; Moses did not think of the heavens having literal gates that could be shut and then opened to let the rain out. In Psalm 18:2 there are four or five metaphors in this one verse.

ALLEGORY

An allegory is a long metaphor in the form of a story; it describes one subject in words that more exactly belong to another. The passage we used in the previous chapter from Judges 9:8–15 is an allegory. When we know this, we shall avoid thinking that Jotham really believed the trees talked together. When in John 10:1–16 Jesus spoke of himself in terms of the Good Shepherd, he was using an allegory. Paul used an allegory in Galatians 4:21–31 when he wrote about Sarah and Hagar; in verse 24 he concluded, 'These things may be taken figuratively' and the Greek word he used is the word from which we get our word 'allegory'. We are at liberty to use Bible stores as allegories, just as Paul did, but when we do, we must beware of using them to prove a point. Allegories are only illustrations; they are not the authority for a statement. The rule for the use of illustrations applies equally to allegories.

ANTHROPOMORPHISM

'Anthropomorphism' means to give something the characteristics of a person. When we are speaking of spiritual things we have to use human language. We can only understand about God by using human words, and we frequently refer to God as if he had the ordinary characteristics of a human being. He is, of course, far greater than that. In Isaiah 59:1, 'Surely the arm of the Lord is not too short to save, nor his ear too dull to hear', it would be ignorance of the rules of hermeneutics to suggest God has a huge hand and ear invisibly extended from heaven to earth. There is a similar example in James 5:4 which refers to 'the ears of the Lord Almighty'. From a misunderstanding of this and the 'image of God' in Genesis 1:27, Mormons believe that God has flesh and bones as we have.

HYPERBOLE

Hyperbole is an exaggeration used to make a statement more forceful. When children claim, 'There were millions of people at church this morning', we do not punish them for lying, because we know they are using hyperbole. God used a hyperbole to Abraham when he promised that the Israelites would be as numerous 'as the dust of the earth' (Genesis 13:16). Similarly, in Judges 7:12 the camels of the armies of the Midianites and Amalekites 'could no more be counted than the sand on the seashore'. In Deuteronomy 1:28 the spies reported that the cities of the Amorites were large 'with walls up to the sky'. The use of hyperbole is common, especially in the Old Testament.

LITOTES

Litotes is not a well-known figure of speech, though it is well used. Litotes is a way of confirming the truth of something by denying its opposite. If I am asked whether I plan to go out today, I may simply say 'yes', or I may use litotes and say, 'I will not stay indoors.' I have said 'Yes', by saying 'No' to the opposite.

An example of how important it can be to recognize litotes is found in Revelation 3:5. Some Christians think that the expression: 'I will never blot out his name from the book of life,' implies that it is possible for a Christian to lose salvation when God blots out a name from the book of life. This interpretation runs counter to the many assurances in the Bible of eternal salvation; for example John 10:28 and Romans 8:33–39. The book of Revelation is full of figures of speech and this phrase is simply an example of litotes: God is confirming the impossibility of something by saying 'No' to the opposite.

APOCALYPTIC LANGUAGE

Some of the picture language that is used in the Bible to refer to the fulfilment of prophecies is strange, and often hard for us to understand. This is referred to as 'apocalyptic' language. That word comes from a Greek verb meaning 'to reveal' or 'bring to light'. At times, we may think the passage does anything but reveal or bring to light. However, we often complicate these Bible pictures. This is especially true in some of the visions of Daniel, where the explanation is given (see Daniel 7:23; 8:19, for example). But on other occasions we are left wondering.

A wise principle is to accept that we do not have to understand every detail of these visions and dreams. It is best to think of them as images that are intended to create an impression of power, or glory, terror, or judgement; our task is to decide first what that impression is. The book of Revelation loses much of its confusion and gains deep significance if we look at it in this way. We can often miss the overall impression because we are too busy examining the detail. Seven is a number of perfection, 144,000 a symbol of completeness and so on. In a book like Revelation—so full of pictures and symbols—it is unwise to take any of the numbers as necessarily representing a fixed amount, either of people or years. Once again, we must be careful not to pick and choose; if we take almost all the numbers as symbols, it is inconsistent hermeneutics to take an occasional one literally because it suits our particular doctrine.

Even when apocalyptic language is hard to understand it can still be very meaningful.

Understanding the parables

A parable is another figure of speech. The Greek word for 'parable' means 'to throw or place by the side of something.' Someone has described them as earthly stories with a heavenly meaning, but that is too simplistic, because many of them have a decidedly earthly meaning. Most of the prophets used parables, but we will limit our comments here to those of Jesus. It is worth keeping in mind that the word 'parable' (*parabolē*) is used also for what we would call a proverb (eg Luke 4:23). In recent years there has been a lot of discussion about how we should interpret the parables of Christ, so we will begin with a little history!

Under the influence of Greek philosophy, in the early days of the Christian church it was not only the parables that were allegorized, but the whole Bible and especially the Old Testament. This meant reading spiritual lessons from every part of a parable. Augustine, who was bishop at Hippo in North Africa from 396 to 430, set the pace for this approach to the parables. In his interpretation of the Good Samaritan (Luke 10:30–37), the wounded man is Adam, Jerusalem is heaven, the thieves represent the devil and his agents, the priest and Levite are the Old Testament law (which cannot save), the Samaritan is Christ (who alone can save), the inn is the church, and the innkeeper is the apostle Paul. Others added that the oil and wine represent baptism and the Lord's Supper—or perhaps the two coins represented these?

The problem with treating the parables like this is that no two interpreters agree on the details, and it leaves us free to read anything we wish into the teaching of Jesus.

- Parables are simple, often vivid and gripping stories, so there have to be details that simply help the narrative along which have no other purpose than that. The stories are designed to capture the listeners' attention and to draw them into the story as participants.

- Jesus himself made an important comment about his parables: 'The secret of the kingdom of God has been given to you. But to those on the outside everything is said in parables so that "they may be ever seeing but never perceiving, and ever hearing but never understanding; otherwise they might turn and be forgiven."' (Mark 4:11–12). Here, Jesus was quoting from Isaiah 6:9–10. Later we read, 'With many similar parables Jesus spoke the word to them, as much as they could understand. He did not say anything to them without using a parable. But when he was alone with his own disciples, he explained everything' (vv. 33–34). In other words, through the parables Jesus taught the secrets of the Kingdom of God—how God rules and works.

- Some things are hidden within parables that will only be plain to those with spiritual understanding. That is why Jesus expected his disciples to be able to understand them. This does not mean we can let our imagination run wild.
- The context is important. To whom was Jesus speaking? Why? What was the result? Sometimes the context gives us the explanation of the parable; this is true of the parable of the seeds in Luke 8:5–15, where Jesus gave his disciples a full interpretation and at the same time left us with some important guidelines as to how parables should be understood. The context may direct our attention to the exact purpose of the parable. This happens in the parable of the Good Samaritan, which answered the question raised in Luke 10:29 'Who is my neighbour?'
- Generally, there is one main point to each parable. This is a wise rule to start with, even though there may be secondary lessons in a parable. Some parables are simple and require little explanation. For example, the parable of the lost sheep in Luke 15:3–7 teaches the one point that there is rejoicing in heaven over each sinner who repents (v. 7). We may also see that there is care by the shepherd who comes looking for the lost sheep, but that is a subsidiary lesson. We cannot go further, or else we might complain at his neglect of the other ninety-nine!
- There are more complex parables that are explained for us. The parable of the seed sown (Mark 4) is one example of this. We are unwise to go beyond the interpretation Jesus himself gave, and we may assume that

he has given us all we need to know. There are also complex parables that are not explained. In the parable of the talents (Luke 19:12–27) we have a number of characters in the story, each of which has to be applied: the nobleman, the servants—some good and some bad—and the citizens, who were all bad. The context helps us here, since it was given just before the triumphal entry into Jerusalem.

- We must be careful not to press every point in a parable. The great danger of spiritualizing (or allegorizing) every part of a parable is that we are left with some parts that are highly embarrassing if we try to apply them. Jesus used everyday and familiar situations in his parables. When he referred to slavery or a dishonest steward (Luke 16:1–15), he was not commenting upon the morality of these situations; they were merely illustrations. Similarly, he does not commend the actions of an unjust judge, or compare him with God (Luke 18:1–8). The point of the story relates not to the judge, but to the woman who kept on and on with her request.

We have not covered all the figures of speech used in the Bible, but the subject is not as difficult as it may appear. Common sense will interpret most figures of speech.

Understanding the New Testament letters

There are twenty-one letters (epistles) in the New Testament, and these are possibly the most used part of our Bible. It is from these letters that we draw most of our Christian teaching. It would be worth checking out Book 1 chapter 5 in this series where the evidence of authentic authorship is considered.

REMEMBER THEY ARE LETTERS

God chose this way to teach us because they were written to real people, in real situations and often to deal with real problems. They are not books of theology disconnected with the reality of life. Paul wrote to be read (Colossians 4:16; 1 Thessalonians 5:27; 2 Thessalonians 3:14, 1 Timothy 4:13) and so did Peter (2 Peter 3:16).

We need to ask, 'Who were the people he was writing to? What kind of Christians were they? Where did they live? What kind of society was it? When did he write? Why did he write? What were the particular problems?' (See, for example, 1 Corinthians 1:11; 3:3; 5:1–2; 7:1; 11:17; 15:12; 16:1 and 1 Thessalonians 4:9; 4:13; 5:1).

Letters are always meant to be understood, so we must look first for the obvious meaning, though there are 'some things that are hard to understand' (2 Peter 3:16). Although they are packed with vital theological truth, they are not handbooks of systematic theology but personal letters, often informal, and were intended to be read at one sitting. The New Testament writers did not divide their letters into chapters and verses—see Book 4 chapter 3 in this series for this. The New Testament letters throb with life and reality. They are not the visionary meditations of a recluse; the writers were men involved with the churches every day. Read carefully those final greetings, for example in Romans 16 and Galatians 4.

LOOK FOR THE BIG THEMES AND DIFFERENT APPROACHES

These letters were not written to be dissected word by word, or even sentence by sentence. What was the writer saying to his day? What has this to say to us? Was there one, or more, big issue that concerned the writer? It is the writer's theme or themes that we must look for, not our interest, or theological hobby-horse.

What was Paul's big theme in Galatians? The true gospel contrasted with the law. But what law? The moral law (the Ten Commandments) or the ceremonial law (sacrifice and offerings) or both? This is an important question to answer. The letter to Rome uses the word 'law' primarily in the sense of the moral law, whilst the letter to the Hebrews uses it with particular reference to the ceremonial law.

The big theme in Ephesians is the unity and one-ness of the Christians—see under 'Paul's theological emphasis' in the previous chapter. Colossians is written to a church in danger of being led astray by 'empty philosophy' (Colossians 2:8). The letters to the Corinthians deal with a range of issues from immoral behaviour, indiscipline in the church, spiritual gifts, the resurrection, and much more. To the Thessalonians, Paul responds to questions about death and the return of Jesus Christ. Hebrews is written to show the supremacy of Jesus as the greatest revelation of God and the fulfilment of the older covenant. James was concerned for those who profess faith but lack the evidence of a Christian life of love. Peter wrote to encourage Christians facing violent persecution, and John clearly had the false teaching of the Gnostics and others in his sights (see Book 3 chapter 8 in this series).

Remember, there was always a purpose in the minds of the apostles when they wrote to individual churches or fellow workers.

Just as Paul preached in different ways in Acts, depending on whether his main audience was Jewish or pagan, so the apostles wrote in different ways. Philemon is a personal letter to a friend asking for a special favour. Romans is written to a church from a pagan background and he must present fundamental Christian theology. The Corinthians were in a real mess, spiritually, morally, theologically, and socially, so needed a firm hand of warning from Paul. Titus needed encouragement as a young pastor/preacher in Crete where the islanders were renowned for being 'liars, evil brutes, lazy gluttons'. Timothy must not be intimidated by his apparent youthfulness. To the Thessalonians Paul expresses his pleasure that they are running well in their Christian and church life and he encourages them to keep on. The Hebrew converts were familiar with Old Testament ceremony, but were not making mature progress in their Christian lives. It is this living variety that makes the New Testament so exciting, and relevant, to read.

GRASP HOW RADICAL WAS THE EARLY CHRISTIAN ETHIC

We touched on this in the previous chapter under, 'The street—the cultural context'. It is worth re-reading that section.

BEWARE OF YOUR OWN THEOLOGICAL BIAS

It is necessary to have a theology, but we should be alert to the fact that this will bias our interpretation of the Bible. Our theological starting point must be formed from Scripture and not from a confession or statement of faith. Once we have a firm grasp of theology from the Bible, we can use that as a lens through which we understand the Bible as a whole. But a caution is needed that our theology is a guide and still we must submit to the full teaching of Scripture.

Because the letter of James lays such stress on the importance of good works as a necessary expression of a Christian faith, Martin Luther, the sixteenth century German Reformer, saw little value in the letter of James; he suggested that it might not be part of the New Testament canon. The reason for this was that he was so preoccupied with proclaiming and defending the vital doctrine of justification by faith alone, that he did not always grasp the importance of good works validating a profession of faith in Christ. His correct theological bias led him to an incorrect understanding of the epistle of James.

It is similarly easy to approach the book of Revelation with a preconceived view of the 'last things'. We have been told just where the 'millennium' fits into the events of the end of the age and we therefore read the whole book, and some of the rest of the Bible, through that lens. It would be far wiser to read the Revelation with the assumption that we are a first century converted pagan with no historical background of millennial views. We quickly appreciate that from chapter four on, we are reading a literature of types and symbols perhaps with little that is intended to be taken literally. That may help us get to grips with the recurring theme of the conflict between Christ and Satan and the final victory of the Redeemer.

Similarly, when reading 1 Timothy 2:3–6; 4:10, 'God… wants all men to be saved… God, who is the Saviour of all men', our starting-point may wisely be to assume that we are Timothy reading this for the first time and without the benefit of Augustine or Arminius, Warfield or Wesley, and perhaps with only Paul's letter to the church at Rome as a background. What did Romans 9:11–21 mean to Christians in the capital city of the Roman empire, in a hard and uncompromising age, and from a pagan background where the will of the gods was dominant, uncontrollable and final?

Understanding the Old Testament—new meanings for old

In addition to looking for the plain and obvious meaning of an Old Testament story, the apostles looked for the principal lesson to be learnt from instructions given in the Old Testament. In 1 Corinthians 9:9 and 1 Timothy 5:18 Paul referred to the regulations in Deuteronomy 25:4 concerning the care of the ox whilst it is treading out the corn. When Paul commented that this was not written for the sake of the animals but for us, he was not denying the plain sense of an Old Testament passage. Whilst recognizing the value of such a verse in relation to animal husbandry, the apostle was more concerned to draw out the deeper application which is that if God is interested in an ox, surely he must be much more interested in our care for Gospel workers. A principle that Jesus also emphasised when he promised that if God is concerned for sparrows, how much more he will be concerned for his children (Matthew 10:29–31).

Similarly, in 2 Corinthians 8:15 Paul referred to the collection of manna in the wilderness (Exodus 16:18) to demonstrate God's principle of equality among Christians.

STORIES AS ILLUSTRATIONS OR ALLEGORIES

It is important to keep in mind the difference between a verse that can be used as an illustration and one that can be used for a text as the authority upon which we can build our teaching. An illustration is only a window to throw light on our subject, but a text is God's declared authority for our subject.

To base a sermon on backsliding on 2 Samuel 14:28, 'Absalom lived two years in Jerusalem without seeing the king's face', is a misuse of Scripture. That verse is simply a statement that David had banished his son Absalom from his presence because Absalom had killed his own brother. We are entitled to use it as an illustration of backsliding: 'Just as Absalom spent two full years in Jerusalem and yet never came into the presence of the king, so the Christian may spend years among God's people and attending church (or far off in the world) and never come close to the presence of the Lord.' In fact, this account is especially intended to teach us how sin breaks relationships within the family.

An excellent sermon was preached on 2 Samuel 9 concerning David's care for Saul's surviving and disabled grandson Mephibosheth. The sermon likened his condition to ours: he was crippled and separated from the king (the results of sin), restored to favour (salvation) and then promoted to eat at the king's table (fellowship with Jesus Christ). It was a good gospel sermon, and included the fact that Mephibosheth, even after his restoration, bore the marks of his fall (he was crippled when his nurse dropped him whilst fleeing from the Philistines). But is this the primary reason why God moved men to record those episodes in Israel's history? To use Old Testament stories as allegories or illustrations of the gospel, is perfectly correct, but an illustration is not our authority; it *proves* nothing. In this case, the theology was perfect, but the hermeneutic was poor. In presenting the story in this way we lost one of the most beautiful records in the Old Testament concerning true loyalty in friendship (to Jonathan), and caring for those who have nothing to offer in return (to Mephibosheth).

Some will respond that the above judgement on this misuse of the Old Testament is an empty approach, merely discovering moral lessons in the Old Testament; we are told that even a Jewish Rabbi can do that. But why should he not? This was God's word for the Jewish Rabbi long before Jesus came. How can it be empty to learn of the disastrous effects of sin, which will point us on to Christ? Or to discover an example of true friendship in the Bible, especially as it will be a simple step to move from here to Christ as the greatest example of friendship?

By contrast, a preacher may use the tragic events of Saul consulting a clairvoyant at Endor (1 Samuel 28) as his biblical authority for warning against all involvement with the world of evil spirits (cf. Deuteronomy 18:9–13).

If we do not distinguish between biblical events that can be used as an illustration and those that can be used as authoritative teaching on a subject we betray our claim to the authority of God's word.

TYPES AND SYMBOLS

The New Testament has an authority—that we do not have—to take us into hidden areas of understanding. Sometimes they wrote of the Old Testament in a fuller way than may be obvious to us from a first reading of the passage. For example, in Matthew 2:15 the Gospel writer understood Hosea 11:1 to be fulfilled in the escape to and return from Egypt by Mary and Joseph with the infant Christ. The natural reading of Hosea is that this refers to the Exodus from Egypt by the children of Israel, but Matthew sees a 'deeper fulfilment' in that passage.

Paul used Hagar and Sarah as an 'allegory'—and that is the actual word he used in the Greek of Galatians 4:24. He also used Adam as a pattern in Romans 5:14, and the rock, manna and the punishment of the people of Israel as examples in 1 Corinthians 10:3,4,6,11. In this passage (and in Romans 5:14) Paul used the word *tupos* or 'pattern'. Similarly, Peter referred to the Flood as an illustration (*antitupon*) of baptism in 1 Peter 3:21. The Day of Atonement is also spoken of as a 'parable' (that is the word used) in Hebrews 9:9.

Several words are used here, and many are interchangeable: allegory, pattern, example, parable, illustration, symbol. But do the apostles over-spiritualize the Old Testament stories? Hagar and Sarah did, quite literally, represent the slave and the free, and Adam clearly was a pattern of Christ since Christ has gained all that Adam lost. The Day of Atonement, and all the Old Testament ceremonies and sacrifices, had no significance apart from Christ (see Galatians 3:24–25) and were clearly types of Christ. We may find the use of the rock and manna unusual, but the word *tupos* that Paul uses has at least six different meanings ranging from an impression, to a copy, pattern, example or symbol. The translation 'example' in 1 Corinthians 10:6,11 is clearly what Paul had in mind.

It may help, for the purposes of understanding the Bible, to distinguish between types and symbols, though it must be stressed that we are here making the distinction of words a little more precise than the New Testament does.

- A *symbol* is something that is used to represent something else. The book of Revelation is full of symbols. The 'beasts' in chapter 13 and 'Babylon' in chapter 17 are two examples among many. Similarly, the prophecies of Daniel and Ezekiel contain many symbols and we must be careful to avoid the temptation to interpret symbols literally. Often (though not always) a symbol does not have any reality in itself; it is merely a picture to describe something else. It is wrong to use biblical symbols as proof-texts. Symbols are closely aligned with illustrations, allegories and parables.

- A *type* on the other hand, has an inseparable connection with the thing it represents. For example, the Tabernacle and all the ceremonies associated with it were given to Israel as a type of the sacrifice of Jesus Christ. They had no meaning or value apart from that to which they pointed.

The difference between the type and the symbol is that symbols are only pictures; in themselves they may have no significance or necessary relationship to the subject they are illustrating. On the other hand, a type has as its chief or only function the representation of that to which it points. When Paul referred to Sarah and Hagar to illustrate a point in Galatians 4 he readily appreciated that these two women had purposes in Scripture other than merely to illustrate his point and he therefore admitted in verse 24 'this may be interpreted allegorically' (ESV). The NIV uses the word 'figuratively'.

This distinction is not always easy to follow, but it is important. We cannot use the account of Abraham and Isaac found in Genesis 22 as a type of the Father sending his Son to die. There may be similarities between this and God's sacrifice of his only Son, but this is not the chief purpose, or any purpose, of that story. We may use it as an illustration of the Gospel, but it is an imperfect illustration because, in the event, Abraham did not have to fulfil his willingness to sacrifice his son. The main purpose in Genesis 22 is to focus on the unquestioning obedience of Abraham because of his unshakable confidence in the God who can raise the dead (Hebrews 11:19).

Without this careful distinction, we could 'discover' types everywhere in the Old Testament, and that would make nonsense of a sound understanding of the Bible. To call Jonah a type of Christ may lead us into the danger of trying to find many other comparisons and it will not be long before we are suggesting that Jonah's attempted escape from God's will is a picture of Christ in Gethsemane—that would lead into a completely false view of Gethsemane. To express this another way: we may work back from Jesus to Jonah (as Jesus himself did), but we cannot work forward from Jonah to Jesus.

Similarly, the story of Joseph is never, in the Bible, spoken of as a type of Christ, and the time we spend on his life trying to discover all the parallels with the life of Christ would be far better employed learning the many lessons about living a godly life in an alien culture and trusting God in both adversity and prosperity; there is a direct application from the life of Joseph to the life of any Christian. To deal with him in any other way is to miss the main point of the record.

It may sound spiritual to 'find Christ in all the Scriptures' but that can lead to some strange interpretations of the Bible and miss the vital moral and spiritual instructions God has for his people in all ages. On the other hand, even if we are not expected to 'find' Christ everywhere, we can, and should, 'reach' him everywhere. Joseph may not be a type or even illustration of Christ, but tracing the record of Joseph's life must lead us to the forgiveness and transformation that is available in Jesus.

Beware the peddlers!

Paul warned the Christians at Corinth against those who use the Scriptures to their own ends, often for material gain and no more: 'Unlike so many, we do not peddle the word of God for profit. (2 Corinthians 2:17). Among those who acknowledge the Bible to be God's word, there will always be those who in practice deny this belief by their action in mishandling Scripture.

- While the main message of the Bible is plain for even a child to understand, there are difficult passages that have puzzled commentators throughout the centuries. Beware those with instant solutions to every problem, who are supremely self-confident in understanding 'the spirits in prison' (1 Peter 3:19) and the 'man of lawlessness' (2 Thessalonians 2:3). Some of the modern cults assume they have the final explanation for every difficult passage of prophecy in the Bible and the Mormons claim that Paul's statement concerning those who are 'baptised for the dead' in 1 Corinthians 15:29—a statement that has mystified the most scholarly and spiritual commentators—is 'unambiguous'. On their assured interpretation of this verse they have built a huge doctrine of baptism on behalf of others.[16]

There is no shame in admitting that we do not fully understand a particular passage of Scripture. Peter found some things in Paul's letters 'hard to understand' and commented that these were the very parts 'which ignorant and unstable people distort' (2 Peter 3:16). No one can be an expert in every part of Scripture. Hermeneutics requires a prayerful life, careful thought, diligent study, and a humble admission on the 'tight points' that we may be wrong.

- Periodically, someone 'discovers' something new in the Bible that the Christian church has apparently never seen before. Almost all the modern cults began like this: it was their special understanding of the 'visions' of their founder, or the vital importance of one aspect of the Bible.

  However, this is not confined to the cults. Evangelical theologians are in the habit of presenting 'new' perspectives that necessitate a detailed analysis of the Scriptures beyond the ability of most of us to follow. As a contemporary example, we can follow the attempts to reinterpret the early chapters of Genesis and avoid a six-day creation. An ever-increasing number of new suggestions have emerged. In the nineteenth century, the 'Day-age theory' was suggested and in the twentieth century the 'Revelatory day theory' and the 'Gap theory' were offered. Into the twenty-first century the 'Framework hypothesis' was popular and more recently the 'Cosmic Temple theory' (or Creation Functionality view) is going the rounds. We have 'New Perspectives' on the law of God, Justification by Faith, and much more. We are right to be at least a little cautious before accepting interpretations that centuries of wise, spiritual, and scholarly Bible commentators have apparently never imagined.

  It is probably wise to pass by and leave the theologians to quibble over new theories until they are either proven to be well founded, are overtaken by something newer than new, or disappear along with so many other theological novelties. When the Bible warns, 'There is

16 *Articles of Faith*. The doctrinal statements of the Church of Jesus Christ of Latter-Day Saints (Mormonism), p. 149, 'These words are unambiguous.'

nothing new under the sun' (Ecclesiastes 1:9) it is a helpful reminder that if something is new, it is probably not true, and if it is true, it is probably not new. If a way of interpreting a passage cannot be found in any commentary, perhaps this is because it has been tried and rejected long ago. We must never be intimidated by scholarship. Any theory of interpreting Scripture that demands a knowledge and skill well beyond that of the ordinary Christian is suspect.

- One great danger facing teachers and preachers of the Bible is that of adding to a Bible narrative to make the telling of it more effective. It is important to read carefully all that is said in the Bible and to include everything that Scripture tells us. It is also often helpful to add background details of geography, customs, and the world scene around Judaea that will set the story in its context. It is also perfectly in order to add a few suggestions of what may or may not have taken place or how those in the account may have responded.

  However, the danger for any good story-teller with a bright imagination, is that these 'extras' can be offered in such a way that they are indistinguishable from the facts in the biblical account. Adding long and imaginative events to the biblical record, weaving them in so that the hearer thinks they are really part of the true narrative, is both dishonest and misleading. Worse still, is then to apply lessons from those imaginative additions as if they had God's authority behind them. This abuse of Scripture, however ignorantly or well-meaning it may be done, is indefensible.

Conclusion

The Bible is God's book and it has his stamp of authority across it. His word is authoritative—not our particular interpretation of it. God has given us rules by which we can rightly understand his word. They are not hard to follow and they are within the reach of everyone who prayerfully and carefully uses them as a key to interpret this treasure box. Interpret the Bible sensibly and spiritually. Make it relevant, not ridiculous. Ask for the help of God's Holy Spirit, because he is the reliable interpreter of his own book. And enjoy your Bible!

4. Getting to grips with the Old Testament

This outline can be downloaded as a PDF. Go to https://www.dayone.co.uk/collections/books/all-you-need-to-know

The following outline of the Old Testament follows the history chronologically. The 'Preparation for Christ' indicates some of the main Old Testament texts that prepare for the coming of the Messiah. The fullest treatment of this subject can be found in the work of Ernst Wilhelm Hengstenberg *Christology of the Old Testament*. Hengstenberg was a German Lutheran pastor, theologian and tutor in Oriental languages at Basel. He was a prolific author and his three volumes on this subject were published between 1829 and 1835. The page numbers in brackets refer to the English translation published by MacDonald Publishing Company, McLean, Virginia, USA. For a more accessible treatment of this subject, a helpful guide is Walter C Kaiser Jr *The Messiah in the Old Testament* (Zondervan Publishing House, Grand Rapids 1995).

You will notice how the prophecies become more specific and clear as the time of the Messiah's birth draws closer. From the general promise to Adam and Eve and the broad sweep of a nation and family (2000 BC), to the specific details of the Messiah (700 BC) and the events of world powers in preparation (500 BC).

The word *Messiah* is a Hebrew word and means the 'Anointed One'. It is used as an adjective or noun around 40 times in the Old Testament (mainly in Samuel and Psalms) and almost always for a king. It is even used of Cyrus of Persia (Isaiah 45:1) as the chosen king for the sake of the people of God. In its immediate context Psalm 2:2 probably refers to the chosen king of Israel, but from Acts 13:32 and Hebrews 1:5; 5:5 it clearly also has a Messianic reference. Some psalms may have the dual reference, but others may be exclusively Messianic because the deity of the Messiah is in focus, for example 45:6-7, cf. Hebrews 1:8-9; 102:25-27, cf. Hebrews 1:10-12; 110:1, cf. Hebrews 1:13.

An outline of the Old Testament and how God unfolded his plan for the coming of Jesus Christ

Bible ref.	Approx. date	Main content	Preparation for Christ
GENESIS 1 to 11	Before 2000 BC	The Creation. **Adam** and Eve. The Fall. The murder of Abel. God's choice of Seth. The founding of the nations. Babel and the Flood.	The first promise of Christ: 3:15. The first recorded prayer to God: 4:26. The first plan of election: 4:25; 5:3, 29. The promise of God's faithfulness: 9:13–16.
11 to 25	2091 BC 2066	The family of **Abraham**. His call to leave Haran. Abraham in Canaan and Egypt. His separation from Lot. The birth of Ishmael. Destruction of Sodom and Gomorrah. The birth and offering of **Isaac**. Rebekah. Abraham's change of name (17:5).	A special people: 12:2; 18:18. A special purpose: 12:3. A special protection: 12:3. A special land: 12:7. A special descendant: 18:17–18, cf. Gal. 3:14, 16; Rom. 4:13. 16:7: The appearance of the 'angel of the LORD' to Hagar. An expression referring to a pre-incarnation appearance of Christ—see also 32:1–24. See also where the Angel is referred to: 12:7; 17:1; 18:17; 21:17; 28:13;
25 to 26	2006	The birth of Jacob and Esau. The death of Abraham.	48:16. See later Josh. 5:13–15 and especially Judges. Hengstenberg comments that the early Jews all understood the Angel of the LORD as 'the one mediator between God and the world, the author of all revelation' (p. 1308). Here his deity is also revealed. See also in Zech. 3:1; 12:8; etc. The promises renewed to Isaac: 26:4. The choice of Jacob: 25:23.

27 to 35 36		The story of **Jacob (Israel)**. The great deceit. His exile and dream at Bethel. Living with Laban, Rachel and Leah The descendants of Esau.	The promise renewed to Jacob: 28:13–15.
37 to 50	1898 1805	Joseph. Slave, prisoner, Egyptian official. The famine in Egypt. Joseph's sons. Jacob comes to Egypt. **Judah** and the death of Jacob and Joseph. Between Genesis 50 and Exodus 1 there are 430 silent years of Israel's slavery in Egypt: Gen. 15:13; Exod. 12:40.	The promise passed on through Judah: 49:8–12; cf. Rev. 5:5. The Hebrew of 49:10 is literally 'until Shiloh comes', with 'Shiloh' referring to 'rest'. A reference to the Messiah as the man of rest, cf. Isa. 9:5–7 (p. 45).
EXODUS 1 to 12		'Exodus' means 'the way out'. We are introduced to the oppression of the Hebrews in Egypt and the birth of Moses. Moses is forced into exile and returns to lead the people. The plagues and **Passover**.	The Passover, with its sacrificial lamb and sprinkled blood, pointed to Christ: Exod. 12:1–14; John 1:29; Luke 22:8, 15, 19–20; 1 Cor. 5:7.
13 to 18	1526	**The Exodus** and miracle at the Red Sea. The desert of Shur and the waters of Mara. Elim and the desert of Sin (quails and manna). Rephidim and the battle with the Amalekites.	
19 to 31	1446	**Mt Sinai** and the Ten Commandments (three months out of Egypt). God gives Moses plans for living (20–30) and worshipping (24–31).	The purpose of the law was to take charge of us and lead us to Christ: Gal. 3:24; Rom. 4:15; 10:4.
32 to 34		Aaron and the golden calf. Moses prays for the people and the law is renewed.	
35 to 40		The tent of meeting (tabernacle). Gifts offered and the priests and others employed.	

LEVITICUS 1 to 7 8 to 10 11 to 22 23 to 27		The laws for the tribe of Levi, the priests. The various **sacrifices and offerings**. The ordination and ministry of **Aaron and the priests**. Nadab and Abihu Regulations for moral, ceremonial and physical cleanness. **Festivals**, rewards and punishments, the law of redemption.	The whole book is pointing forward to Christ. The Aaronic priesthood, the Levites, the tabernacle and its implements, and the various sacrifices and ceremonies were all a preparation for Christ, the Messiah. We may therefore refer to 'the gospel according to Leviticus'. The book reveals two great facts: (1) The quality of sacrifice: perfect. (2) The cost of sacrifice: death.
NUMBERS		From Sinai to the desert of Paran. Two years and two months out from Egypt.	
1 to 9		A census of the people. Duties of the Levites and the dedication of the tabernacle.	
10 to 12		The people leave Sinai and complain. Aaron and Miriam rebel.	
13 to 14		Spies are sent to Canaan. The people lack faith to go forward.	
15 to 19		Various duties and the rebellion of Korah.	
20 to 21		Water from the rock. The disobedience of Moses and later of the people. The bronze snake.	Paul uses the rock as an analogy of Christ in 1 Cor. 10:4. The snake on the pole was a symbol of Christ on the cross: John 3:14.
22 to 25		Moab and the false prophet, Balaam.	In 24:17–19 the false prophet, Balaam, nevertheless looks on to the Messianic age by reference to the star and sceptre—cf. Gen. 49:10. The ancient Jews saw this as a promise of David and then the Messiah (p. 67).
26 to 30		Another census. Offerings and festivals.	

31 to 36		Destruction of the Midianites. Campsites though Sinai. Levite towns and cities of refuge.	
DEUTERONOMY		The title means 'the second law'. The scene is forty years out of Egypt, in the land of Moab, at the border of the Promised Land.	
1 to 26		Moses recounts the story of the wanderings from Mt Sinai, forty years before. He includes their rebellion and disobedience, and his own failure. The Ten Commandments are given a second time and Moses urges the people to remain faithful to God. He passes on to them various laws from God.	18:15–19: this 'prophet' was understood by the ancient Jews, the early church and many Reformers to be Messianic (p. 72). See Acts 3:22–23; 7:37; John 1:46; 5:45–47; Luke 24:44. This is the prophet alluded to in John 4:25–26.
27 to 31		Mts Gerizim and Ebal: Blessings for obedience and judgement for disobedience. The covenant renewed.	
32 to 34	1406	Moses' final sermon. The appointment of Joshua as his successor. A song of praise and his blessing on the tribes. The death of Moses.	
JOSHUA 1 to 5		Joshua takes command on the death of Moses. Spies are sent out, the Jordan crossed and preparations made for war.	5:13–15: compare the 'commander of the army of the LORD' with Christ's claim in Matt. 26:53. See also the angel going before Israel in Exod. 23:20–23 (33:15–16); cf. Isa. 63:9. The crossing of the sea, the pillar of cloud, the rock from which water flowed, and the manna are pictures of Christ: Deut. 32:18; 1 Cor. 10:1–4; John 6:30–33.

6 to 10:28		The central campaign: (1) Jericho and Ai. The sin of Achan. (2) Deceit and rescue of the Gibeonites. (3) The long day at Gibeon.	
10:29–43 11 12 to 19 20 to 22		The southern campaign. The northern campaign. A list of defeated kings and land still unpossessed. Division of the land among the twelve tribes. Cities of refuge and Levite cities.	Judah inherits Jerusalem: 15:63.
23 to 24	1356	Joshua's final charge to the Israelites. The covenant renewed. The death of Joshua.	The people are reminded of the promises to the patriarchs and they pledge their allegiance to the LORD. There is no mention of the Messiah at this point, although he is assumed within the promises to Abraham. Israel's pledge of loyalty is short-lived.
JUDGES 1 to 2	1356 to 1050	The judges, or deliverers, who led Israel for 300 years. There were 15 judges (Eli and Samuel are in 1 Samuel). This is possibly the most tragic book in the Bible. It is the 'dark ages' of the Bible, 2:7,10 explaining the recurring theme of rest, rebellion, retribution, repentance, restoration. 2:11–19 describes the sad cycle of events. Nevertheless, there are some outstanding men and women of faith: Heb. 11:32.	Judges is a record of Israel's unfaithfulness. There is no prophecy of the coming Messiah in the book. The line leading to the Messiah is obscured by sin. However, the 'Angel of the LORD' (see 2:1–3) appears fifteen times and speaks more often here than in any other Old Testament book. The Messiah is active though unrecognized (pp. 80–90).

CHAPTERS	YEARS	JUDGE	OPPRESSOR	YEARS	EVENTS
3	40	Othniel	Cushan of Aram (Mesopotamia)	8	
	80	Ehud	Eglon of Moab	18	Assassination of Eglon.
		Shamgar	Philistines		Shamgar killed 600 with an ox-goad.
4 to 5	40	Deborah	Jabin of Canaan	20	Assassination of Sisera, Jabin's commander.
6 to 8	40	Gideon	Midianites and Amalekites	7	Destruction of Baal idol. Gideon's fleece and 300 men.
9	3	Abimelech			Abimelech murdered his 70 brothers.
10 to 11	23	Tola			
	22	Jair			
	6	Jephthah	Philistines and Ammonites	18	
12					Civil war with Ephraim. 'Shibboleth'.
	7	Ibzan			
	10	Eglon			
	8	Abdon			
13 to 16	20	Samson	Philistines	40	Samson's birth, marriage, wars and death.
17 to 21		A catalogue of anarchy: (1) Idolatry of Micah and the Danites. (2) Immorality of the Benjamites. (3) Civil war between Israel and the Benjamites.			
RUTH		Ruth is set in the period of the Judges, possibly during chapters 17–21. An account of the family of Naomi and her Moabite daughter-in-law, Ruth.			A valuable record of the 'thin red line' of the Messiah preserved during the darkest period of Israel's history. Boaz is a 'kinsman-redeemer' (4:14) and the great-grandfather of King David (4:17–22). Its purpose is to demonstrate that, in the darkest period of Israel's history, God was preserving his chosen line for the coming of Christ.

1 SAMUEL	1070 to 970	The main characters of these two books are **Eli and Samuel**, the last of the judges, and **Saul and David**, the first of the kings.	There are no direct prophecies of the coming Messiah. However, God is preparing for the line of David, the ancestor of David's greater Son.
1 to 3		The birth and call of Samuel. Eli and his worthless sons.	
4 to 6		The Philistines capture the ark of the covenant. The death of Eli. God punishes the Philistines and they return the ark.	
7		Samuel as judge. His circuit: Bethel, Gilgal, Mizpah, Ramah (7:15–17).	
	1070	The defeat of the Philistines at Mizpah.	
8 to 11		The people ask for a king. Saul is privately anointed by Samuel. Saul's first battle at Jabesh Gilead, resulting in his public coronation.	
12	1050	Samuel's farewell speech.	
13 to 15		The rout of the Philistines at Michmash and the bravery of Jonathan. The sparing of Agag and Saul's rejection by God.	
16 to 27		David is anointed by Samuel. David and Goliath. Saul's envy of David. David the outlaw and friend of Jonathan. During these years David wrote some of his finest psalms.	Compare 16:1 with Ruth 4:21–22. The line of Boaz, from the tribe of Judah, to a simple shepherd boy, to introduce David the king: the great ancestor of the Messiah.
28 to 31		Saul and the necromancer of Endor and Saul's death on the battlefield.	
2 SAMUEL			
1 to 5	1010	David is king at Hebron until he captures Jerusalem.	
6 to 7		David is established as king and the ark is brought to Jerusalem. God's special promises to David. David's great prayer.	Although 7:5–16 points immediately to Solomon, the promises go beyond this. Verse 13 looks to the reign of the Messiah. For the 'Name' see Exod. 3:15; 6:3; 23:21.

		God's promises to the king and David's prayer.	Many of David's psalms are 'Messianic'. See introduction above. For example: (1) The Sonship of the Messiah: 2:2.
8 to 10 9		David at war. David and his kindness to Mephibosheth.	(2) The Suffering Messiah: Ps. 22. (3) The Sovereign Messiah: Ps. 45:6–7; 102:25–27; 110:1.
10 to 12		David's success at war and failure at home. Bathsheba and Uriah. Nathan the prophet. Psalm 51 written at this time.	Heb. 1:5–13 quotes from Ps. 2:7; 45:6–7; 102:25–27; 110:1; and 2 Sam. 7:14.
13 to 19		Amnon and Tamar, and the exile, rebellion and death of Absalom. Psalm 63 possibly written at this time.	
20 to 21		The rebellion of Sheba and vengeance of the Gibeonites.	
22		A psalm of praise by David when he was delivered from Saul.	
23		David's final prophecy and a list of the members of his bodyguard.	David's final prophecy, with its reference to the Rock and the everlasting covenant, also points forward to Christ: 23:1–7.
24		David counts the people and builds an altar. The death of David is recorded in 1 Kings 2:10–11 and 1 Chr. 29:26–30.	
1 KINGS to 2 CHRONICLES	970–587	This period of just under 400 years covers a major part of Bible history and prophecy. The period from the reign of Solomon to the destruction of Jerusalem and exile of the Jews takes up four history books (1–2 Kings; 1–2 Chronicles), four poetry or wisdom books (Proverbs, Ecclesiastes, Song of Songs, plus some of the Psalms), and fourteen prophecy books (Isaiah to Zephaniah). This is more than half the Old Testament.	

		As the title implies, Kings is the story of the kings of Judah and Israel. Chronicles repeats the history of Kings, often in the same words, but looks more at the spiritual history.	
1 Kings 2 to 11		The reign of Solomon and the building of the temple.	The temple replicated all the ceremonial implements from the tabernacle and therefore continued the preparation for the final sacrifice and priesthood of the Messiah.
1 Kings 12 to 2 Kings 25		Rehoboam and the division of the kingdom. Rehoboam in the south (Judah) with Jerusalem as capital. Jeroboam in the north (Israel) with Samaria as capital. There were 20 kings in the north until Samaria was destroyed by Assyria in 722. There were 20 kings (discounting the usurper queen Athaliah) in the south until Jerusalem was destroyed by Babylonia in 587. Many early prophets, from Ahijah to Elijah and Elisha, preached chiefly to Israel. Two outstandingly evil kings in the north were Ahab and Jeroboam II, though all the northern kings mixed pagan worship with that of the Lord. Half of the southern kings were good, though Rehoboam, Ahaz, and Manasseh compromised worship. Hezekiah and Josiah saw periods of vigorous spiritual life and reform.	Through the southern kings in Jerusalem God preserves the line of David in preparation for the Messiah.

PROPHETS	KINGS (An asterisk refers to those who are named in pagan records outside the Bible)				
	Judah (20 kings in Jerusalem)		**Israel** (20 kings in Samaria)		
1 Kings 17 to 2 Kings 9 The preaching of Elijah, Elisha, Obadiah. Micah Joel Amos, Jonah Hosea	Rehoboam	930–913	Jeroboam I	930–909	
	Abijah	913–911	Nadab	910–909	
	Asa	911–869	Baasha	908–886	
			Elah	886–885	
			Zimri	885	
			Omri*	885–874	
	Jehoshaphat	870–848	Ahab*	874–853	
			Ahaziah	853–852	
			Joram	852–851	
	Jehoram (Joram)	846–841	Jehu*	841–814	
	Ahaziah	841			
	Athaliah (usurper queen)	841–835			
	Joash*	835–796	Jehoahaz	814–798	
	Amaziah	796–767	Jehoash*	798–782	
Isaiah prophesied from Azariah to the reign of Hezekiah	Azariah (Uzziah)	767–740	Jeroboam II	782–753	
			Zechariah	753–752	
			Shallum	753–752	
			Menahem*	752–742	
			Pekahiah	742–740	
Micah	Jotham	740–732	Pekah*	740–732	
	Ahaz	732–716	Hoshea*	732–722	The fall of Samaria to Assyria in 722.
	Hezekiah*	716–687			
	Manasseh*	687–642			
Jeremiah	Amon	642–640			
	Josiah	640–608			
	Jehoahaz*	609			
	Jehoiakim (Eliakim)	609–597			
	Jehoiachin*	597			
Ezekiel and Daniel	Zedekiah	597–587			The fall of Jerusalem to Babylon in 597 and 587. Many Jews were exiled to Babylon, including Ezekiel, Daniel and his friends.

OBADIAH	c.848	Obadiah was the first prophet whose ministry is given a Bible book to itself. He prophesied against Edom in the time of Jehoram, king of Judah.	Obadiah reminded Edom that salvation is found only in the God of Judah. Verses 17–21 may have a partial fulfilment in the return from exile in 539, but its ultimate fulfilment is in the kingdom of the Messiah.
JOEL	c.800	Joel preached to Judah in the time of Joash; through the vivid picture of a locust plague he warned of judgement. But Joel looked beyond, to the coming of the Holy Spirit.	Joel 2:23, 'the autumn rains in righteousness', is considered by most of the older commentators to be translated 'Teacher of righteousness'. No matter how this verse is translated, 2:28–3:21 is clearly looking forward to Pentecost and beyond, to the end of the age. In Acts 2:16–21 Peter saw its fulfilment in the cross and Pentecost. The ancient Jews saw Joel as Messianic (p.240).
JONAH	c.796	In the time of Amaziah, Jonah was sent to Nineveh, the capital of Assyria.	Jonah was an illustration of the Messiah: Matt.12:39–41.
NAHUM	642	150 years after Jonah, Nahum prophesied the destruction of Nineveh, and 30 years later the Babylonians fulfilled the prophecy in 612 BC.	A reminder that, ultimately, all who oppose God and his chosen people will meet with his severe judgement.
AMOS	c.782	Although in the time of Amaziah and Uzziah, Amos preached mainly to Israel in the time of Jeroboam II. A warning against disobedience, illustrated by the surrounding nations and prophetic pictures.	9:11–15 look forward to the age of the Messiah's ultimate kingdom. See Acts 15:16–18.
HOSEA	c.767	A contemporary of Amos in the time of Uzziah, Jotham, Ahaz and Hezekiah. Hosea lived through the fall of Samaria in 722. He speaks on behalf of God against Israel's unfaithfulness, which is illustrated by an unfaithful wife.	3:5: After all the unfaithfulness of Israel and Judah, under the picture of an unfaithful wife, the promise is for the Messiah as 'David their king'.

MICAH		Micah was a contemporary of Hosea and Isaiah.	Micah's prophecies are radiant with the glory of the coming Messiah and the redeemed church. The promises of the 'latter days' are to be taken to signify the time of the Messiah. (1) 4:1–8: The kingdom of God will, in the future, be exalted above all the kingdoms of the world. In these verses is also a beautiful picture of the effect of the gospel when the Messiah comes; cf. Zech. 3:10. (2) 5:1–2: Here 'the reference to the Messiah was, at all times, not the private opinion of a few [Jewish] scholars, but was publicly received and acknowledged with perfect unanimity' (p. 359). cf. John 7:41–42; Matt. 2:6
ISAIAH		Both Isaiah and Micah had strong messages of judgement, but offered hope and restoration, both in the immediate future if the nation repented, and in the ultimate promise of the gospel.	Augustine (5th century AD) claimed that, because of his numerous Messianic prophecies, Isaiah deserved the name 'evangelist' rather than 'prophet'. The following are only some of the most pronounced Messianic prophesies in Isaiah; almost all of them were seen as Messianic by Jews—until Christ came, after which they were reinterpreted! 2:2–5: The ultimate glory of the Messiah's kingdom. 7:14–16: Immanuel and the virgin birth as a sign. 9:1–7: A child is born who will reign, cf. Matt. 4:15–16. This whole passage was always treated as Messianic by the ancient Jews (p. 453).

			11–12: The Branch of Jesse; cf. Rom. 15:12; Rev. 5:5; 22:16.
			28:16: The 'cornerstone'; cf. Ps. 118:22; Matt. 21:42–44; Rom. 10:11; 1 Pet. 2:6–7.
			33:17: The future gospel.
			35:5–10: The miracles of Christ; cf. Luke 14:13–21; Matt. 15:31; etc.
			40:1–5: The preparation for the Messiah by John the Baptist; cf. Matt. 3:3.
			42:1–4: The life and ministry of the Messiah; cf. Luke 2:32; Matt. 3:17; 2 Pet. 1:17.
			50:4–11: For the Messiah's obedient life; cf. Matt. 26:67–68; Luke 18:31–32.
			52:13 to 53:12: No passage is used more frequently in the New Testament than this, with eleven quotations and eight allusions. In the Christian church, 'this passage was always considered to be the most distinct and glorious of all Messianic prophecies' (p. 620). Until the coming of Christ, almost all Jewish commentators accepted this passage as Messianic (pp. 613–618).
			60:19–20: cf. Rev. 21:3–4; 22:2–5.
			61:1–3: The Messiah ushers in the time of the LORD's favour; cf. Lk. 4:17–19.

2 KINGS 17	c 732	Hoshea was the last king of Israel. Sargon of Assyria defeated Samaria and thousands were taken into exile, and the land resettled with foreigners.	
ZEPHANIAH	c.640	Zephaniah's preaching encourages the reforms of Josiah of Judah. However, his message is one of foreboding because many of the people are not sincere.	'The Messiah, although not appearing here, stands in the background and forms the invisible centre' (p.648). 3:9–20 refers to the return from exile in 539, but beyond this it reflects the ultimate kingdom of God.
HABAKKUK	c.609	In the time of Jehoahaz. Babylon is the powerful empire. After a dialogue with God pleading Judah's cause, the prophet warns Babylon of her eventual downfall.	2:3: The prophet Habakkuk is told that some of his prophecies will be about the end. And that end is briefly but gloriously described in 2:14. 3:16–19: Even in the face of the terrifying Babylonian army, the prophet is confident in God—a timeless message for God's people.
2 KINGS 24		In 609 Assyria fell to Babylon, whose king, Nebuchadnezzar, attacked Jerusalem, put his own puppet king on the throne and carried many into exile.	
JEREMIAH	c.626	Jeremiah prophesied through the years of the decline of Judah and the two-year siege and destruction of Jerusalem by the Babylonians in 587 BC in the time of Zedekiah. With the capture of Zedekiah, the Hebrew monarchy was at an end. For 50 years the remnant of the people lived almost leaderless in the land. In 592 the governor, Gedaliah, was assassinated and many fled to Egypt to escape reprisals. Jeremiah was taken with them: Jer.42–43.	3:14–17: Jeremiah looks forward to the Messiah and beyond. 23:1–8: The 'Righteous Branch' who will be called 'The LORD Our Righteousness'. 30–31: 'The whole description in both chapters is Messianic', and 31:31–40 is 'the grand hymn of Israel's deliverance' (pp.698, 700). These are the promised days of the Spirit. See also 33:14–26; cf.Heb.10:16–17; John 6:45; 2 Cor.3:3–6.

EZEKIEL	c. 592	Both Ezekiel and Daniel were young contemporaries of Jeremiah and prophesied during the years of exile in Babylon and later under the Persians. Both looked forward to the age of the gospel and the heavenly kingdom. Ezekiel preached against many nations.	The temple in 40–48 is symbolic of the church and the kingdom of God. 'Its fulfilment under the New Testament is constantly going on, and the future alone will witness its completion' (p. 783). For example see 47:3–4: 'We have here a representation of the Messianic salvation which, though at first comparatively insignificant, will continue to expand with ever increasing fullness and glory' (p. 786). Compare 47:10 with Matt. 4:18–19; and 47:12 with Rev. 22:2. In addition, the following are clear Messianic passages: 17:22–24; 34:23–34.
DANIEL		Daniel 1–6 is history and 7–12 is prophecy. Although it is in the Hebrew Scriptures, the book of Daniel is not placed among the prophets. He lived in exile and in high office through six pagan kings. Daniel foretold the kingdoms that would follow from the collapse of the Persian Empire.	2:44 points to the time of the Messiah. 7:13–14: a vision of the 'Son of Man', the Messiah. Jesus frequently described himself like this (e.g. Matt. 8:20 and thirty times in this Gospel). The Jews saw this as Messianic and therefore wrote of the coming Messiah as 'the man of the clouds' (p. 795). 9:25–27: a reference to the final destruction of the temple; cf. Matt. 24:15–16. According to 9:2, Daniel had been studying Jeremiah.
2 CHRONICLES 36		Under Cyrus, the empire of the Medes and Persians defeated the Babylonians.	
EZRA 1–4	c. 539	Cyrus decreed that the exiled nations could return from exile and rebuild their cities and temples. Some Jews returned, but after many problems and much opposition the work halted and the people concentrated on their own homes.	2:59, 62–63 reveals how meticulous was the record keeping of genealogies throughout the history of the Jews. It confirms our trust in the genealogies of Joseph and Mary in Matthew 1 and Luke 3.

HAGGAI		Haggai condemned the people for being more interested in their own comfort than in the temple of God, and he promised a future blessing for the temple.	2:6–9 is a promise of the coming Messiah, before which time the nations will be shaken; cf. Heb. 12:26–28. Calvin explains that 'the condition of the whole world was to be changed by the coming of Christ'. The temple now represents the kingdom of God and the elect will bring the very best to Christ (pp. 944–949).
ZECHARIAH		Zechariah received eight visions which looked forward to the coming of Christ and the age of the gospel.	Zechariah is about little else than Christ; see e.g. 2:10–11; 3:1–10; 6:9–13; 12:10. Compare 9:9 with Matt. 21:5; and 11:12–13 with Matt. 27:9. Each of the visions has a Messianic reference (pp. 965–1182); cf. 3:10 with Mic. 4:4
EZRA 5–10	Sept. 520	The work on the temple recommenced and was completed. Ezra arrived in Jerusalem for the dedication service and effected some necessary reforms. Mixed marriages.	
ESTHER	c. 478	A Jewess who was taken as wife for Ahasuerus (Xerxes) of Persia. She learned of a plot to exterminate the Jews everywhere. Esther pleaded with the king, who intervened, and the Jews were saved. The Jews celebrate this in the annual festival of Purim.	The name of God is not mentioned in the book of Esther, but it is all about his purposes in protecting his chosen people and therefore the line of the Messiah.
NEHEMIAH	445	An officer in the court of Artaxerxes I at Susa in Persia, Nehemiah obtained permission to return to Jerusalem and organize the rebuilding of the city walls. Severe opposition was overcome and Ezra again arrived to take part in the dedication of the walls. Nehemiah returned to court and various abuses crept into city life. A furious Nehemiah returned to the city and carried out reforms.	

MALACHI		Possibly Malachi was preaching during Nehemiah's absence at court. He condemned unholy sacrifices, an unholy priesthood and withholding tithes.	Compare 3:1 and 4:5 with Matt. 11:10–15; 16:13–14—the prophecies of John the Baptist as the herald of the Messiah. It is significant that the Messiah, who is promised at the very beginning of Genesis (3:15), is the subject of the last chapter of the final prophet in the Old Testament.
		There are 400 years of silence in Scripture from the close of Malachi to the opening of Matthew. It is known as the 'Intertestamental Period'.	The fourteen books of the *Apocrypha*—a mixture of history and legend, fact and fantasy—were written during this period. Some of the stories refer to Old Testament events and people, though it also includes the record of the Maccabean wars (167–160 BC). The *Apocrypha* is never quoted in the New Testament. For the *Apocrypha* see Book 3 chapter 2 in this series.

See the next two pages for the period between the Old and New Testaments.

The Intertestamental Period

EMPIRE	DATE		
Persian	539–333	Cyrus defeated the Medes and combined the Medes and Persians into one great empire. In 539 Cyrus conquered Babylon, placed Darius the Mede in charge, and allowed the Jews to return and rebuild their city. His son, Cambyses, pushed the Persian empire from the Nile to India. The biblical record closes around the year 440 with the completion of the city walls of Jerusalem. For two centuries under Persian rule the Jews became a people of the Book (the Torah). The temple in Jerusalem was still the centre of worship, but synagogues grew up among the scattered Jewish communities. The high priest became the political as well as religious leader. Jewish territory extended only 12 to 15 miles around the city and the Jews were economically weak.	Throughout the entire period between the Old and New Testaments there is no visible sign of the 'thin red line' of the redemption plan. Tribal distinctions were blurred and we can only believe that, unseen and unheralded, God was keeping safe the line of the family of the Messiah until the 'time had fully come' (Gal.4:4). However, genealogical records were carefully preserved throughout this period, as Matt.1:12–16 and Luke 3:23–27 reveal. See also Ezra 2:59, 62–63.
Greek	333–323	Alexander the Great defeated the Persians at Issus (northern Syria) in 333. Jerusalem accepted Greek rule without resistance. After the death of Alexander in 323 his empire was carved into a number of rival states: • Macedonia, in northern Greece. • Egypt, the kingdom of the Ptolemies. • The Helespont, under Lysimachus. • Asia Minor and Syria: the Seleucids.	The rapid, though brief, expansion of the Greek empire planted Greek culture across a wide area and Greek became the common language for communication—a vital preparation for the spread of the gospel. Much of Jesus' preaching would have been in Greek, and all the books of the New Testament were written originally in this language of commerce.

Ptolemaic (Egyptian)	323–195	By 311 BC Seleucis I was extending his control. Greek culture (known as Hellenism) was spreading among the Jews. Stadiums were built in the cities and traditional Jews were horrified at the nakedness of the Greek games and the cult of the gods.	Around 250 BC the Old Testament was translated into Greek; it was known as the *Septuagint*. For the *Septuagint* see Book 3 chapter 2 in this series.
Seleucid (Syrian)	195–163	In the reign of Antiochus IV tension flared. In 167 BC hundreds of Hasidim Jews (the 'godly ones') were massacred, the law was destroyed, and the temple and altar were turned over to the cult of Zeus. Pig flesh (abhorrent to the Jews) was offered in the temple and Jews were forced to eat it. The result was the Maccabean wars from 167–160 BC. Judas Maccabeus regained Jerusalem and cleansed the temple and altar. After many brilliant victories, Judas was finally defeated. However, as the Syrian grip declined, the Jews regained their independence, though with factions and bloodshed, until the Romans arrived, and the nationalist cause was lost.	
Roman	from 63 BC	In 63 BC Roman troops entered Palestine and the gates of Jerusalem were opened to them. The Jews were granted control of their internal affairs with a Roman governor. Freedom of worship was guaranteed. In 40 BC the Roman Senate appointed Herod 'King of the Jews', and with the aid of Roman troops he gained control in 37 BC. Herod the Great was a renowned builder, a political adventurer and a cruel tyrant. However, he brought national peace and a degree of prosperity.	A relatively stable government throughout a far-flung empire. Good communication by road and sea provided an excellent preparation for the spread of the gospel.

5. Piecing the Gospels together

There have been many attempts to set out a sequence of events from the four Gospels and none are identical. No Gospel writer claims to present a chronological order.

This harmony of the Gospels can be downloaded as a PDF. Go to https://www.dayone.co.uk/collections/books/all-you-need-to-know

The writers often use expressions like: 'at that time', 'another time', 'one of those days', 'again, Jesus began to teach by the Lake' all of which give little certainty of timing. The phrase 'some time later' (John 5:1), makes it almost impossible to place the events of that chapter. Only with such expressions as 'that same day' or 'immediately after' can we be sure of a sequence. For a suggested order for the last week in the life of Jesus and of the resurrection accounts see *Evidence for the Bible* (Day One Publications) pp. 205–210.

It should also be remembered that a repetition of similar teaching may not have been given at the same time. Doubtless Jesus repeated himself many times.

The outline that follows is this author's own and does not claim to be precise. All passages in the four Gospels are covered.

Main Events	Matthew	Mark	Luke	John
The eternal nature of Jesus				1:1–14
The message of Gabriel to Zechariah			1:1–25	
The birth of John the Baptist and Zechariah's praise			1:57–80	
The genealogy of Jesus	1:1–17		3:23–38	
Gabriel appears to Mary			1:26–38	
The angel appears to Joseph	1:18–25			
Mary visits Elizabeth and Mary's song of praise			1:39–56	
Bethlehem: The birth of Jesus			2:1–7	
The angels appear to shepherds			2:8–20	
Jerusalem: Jesus presented in the temple			2:21–38	
Bethlehem: The visit of the magi	2:1–12			
Egypt: The family escape and the murder of the infants	2:13–20			
Nazareth: The family return home	2:21–23		2:39–40	
Jerusalem: Jesus as a boy questioning the teachers			2:41–52	
The ministry of John the Baptist	3:1–12	1:1–8	3:1–18	1:15–36
The first disciples of Jesus				1:37–51
The baptism of Jesus	3:13–17	1:9–11	3:21–22	
The temptations of Jesus	4:1–11	1:12–13	4:1–13	
Preaching and healing in Galilee				
Jesus' first miracle at Cana in Galilee				2:1–11
Capernaum for a few days				2:12
The Passover in Jerusalem and preaching in Judaea				
The first cleansing of the temple in Jerusalem				2:13–25
A secret meeting with Nicodemus				3:1–21
A 'certain Jew' questions John the Baptist				3:22–36
The woman at the well in Samaria				4:1–42
A return to Galilee				
Jesus' first rejection at Nazareth			4:14–30	

Main Events	**Matthew**	**Mark**	**Luke**	**John**
John the Baptist imprisoned		1:14	3:19–20	
Jesus begins preaching in Galilee	4:12–17, 23–25			
Capernaum: evil spirits and Simon's mother-in-law		1:21–34	4:31–41	
Jesus prays alone and continues preaching in Galilee		1:35–39	4:42–44	
Healing of an official's son at Capernaum				4:43–54
The calling of his disciples and the great catch of fish	4:18–22	1:15–20	5:1–11	
Jesus commissions his twelve disciples		3:13–19	6:12–16	
The sermon on the mount	5:1 to 7:29		6:17–49?	
Healing a man with leprosy	8:1–4	1:40–45	5:12–16	
Capernaum: centurion's servant healed and teaching	8:5–22		7:1–10	
Nain: Widow's son raised			7:11–17	
Capernaum: The paralytic healed and forgiven	9:1–8	2:1–12	5:17–26	
Matthew Levi called to be a disciple	9:9–13	2:13–17	5:27–32	
Questions about fasting	9:14–17	2:18–22	5:33–39	
Healing a sick woman and raising Jairus' daughter	9:18–26	5:21–43	8:40–56	
Healing the blind and mute. The workers are few	9:27–34			
Jesus sends out his twelve disciples	9:35 to 10:42	6:7–12, 30–32	9:1–6	
John's disciples question Jesus	11:1–19		7:18–35	
A woman anoints Jesus in Simon's house			7:36–50	
Parables in Galilee			8:1–21	
Unbelief condemned and Jesus' invitation to rest	11:20–30			
The cornfield, healing and Lord of the Sabbath	12:1–21	2:23 to 3:6	6:1–11	
Jesus accused of exorcising by Beelzebub	12:22–37	3:20–30	11:14–28	
The sign of Jonah	12:38–45		11:29–32	
'Who is my mother?'	12:46–50	3:31–35		
Jesus preaches from a boat	13:1–2	3:7–12		
Parables by the Lake of Galilee	13:3–52	4:1–34		
Nazareth: Jesus' second rejection by his home town	13:53–58	6:1–6		

Main Events	Matthew	Mark	Luke	John
Jesus calms a storm on Galilee	8:23–27	4:35–41	8:22–25	
Healing of the two demon-possessed men	8:28–34	5:1–20	8:26–39	
The death of John the Baptist	14:1–12	6:14–29	9:7–9	
Healing the disabled man at the pool in Jerusalem?				5:1–47
Near Bethsaida: Feeding the five thousand	14:13–21	6:33–44	9:10–17	6:1–15
Jesus walks on the Lake of Galilee	14:22–33	6:45–56		6:16–21
Crowds searching for Jesus				6:22–24
Jesus, the bread of life				6:25–40
Capernaum: The Pharisees grumble against Jesus				6:41–59
Many disciples desert Jesus				6:60–71
Gennesaret: Many healed	14:34–36			
Debating with the Pharisees	15:1–20	7:1–23		
Tyre: The faith of the woman	15:21–28	7:24–30		
Healing a deaf and dumb man		7:31–37		
By Galilee: Feeding the four thousand	15:29–39	8:1–10		
Magadan: the Pharisees demand a sign	16:1–4	8:11–13		
Jesus warns of the yeast of the Pharisees and Sadducees	16:5–12	8:14–21		
Bethsaida: a blind man healed		8:22–26		
Caesarea Philippi: Peter's confession of Christ	16:13–20	8:27–30	9:18–27	
Jesus predicts his coming death	16:21–28	8:31 to 9:1		
Eight days later, the Transfiguration	17:1–13	9:2–13	9:28–36	
Healing the demon-possessed boy	17:14–21	9:14–29	9:37–43	
Passing through Galilee and prediction of his death	17:22–23	9:30–32	9:43–45	7:1–9
Capernaum: the provision of the Temple Tax	17:24–27			
The disciples question who is greatest in the Kingdom	18:1–9	9:33–37	9:46–48	
'Whoever is not against us is for us'		9:38–41	9:49–50	
The millstone warning		9:42–50		
Parable: the lost sheep	18:10–14			
Parables: forgiving a brother; the unmerciful servant	18:15–35			

Main Events	Matthew	Mark	Luke	John
Through Samaria into Judea (Luke 9:51–52)				
On his way to Jerusalem through Samaria			9:51–56	
The cost of discipleship			9:57–62	
Jesus sends out the seventy-two disciples			10:1–24	
The parable of the Good Samaritan			10:25–37	
Ten men healed of leprosy			17:11–19	
Into Judea (Matthew 19:1)				
Bethany: the home of Martha and Mary			10:38–42	
Jerusalem: The Feast of Tabernacles				7:10–52
The woman taken in adultery				7:53 to 8:11
Teaching in Jerusalem				8:12–59
Healing a man born blind				9:1–41
Jesus, the Good Shepherd				10:1–21
The Feast of Dedication				10:22–39
Jesus returns across the Jordan				10:40–42
Bethany: The raising of Lazarus and the Jewish plot				11:1–44
Village of Ephraim: Jesus withdraws from the crowds				11:45–57
Jesus' teaching on prayer			11:1–13	
'Your eye is the lamp'			11:33–36	
Six woes in the home of a Pharisee			11:37–54	
Warnings and encouragements to the crowd			12:1–12	
Parable of the rich fool			12:13–21	
Encouragement not to be anxious but to be watchful			12:22–48	
Warning of division caused by the Gospel			12:49–53	
Interpreting the times			12:54–59	
Necessity of repentance and parable of the fig tree			13:1–9	
A crippled woman healed on the Sabbath			13:10–17	
Parables of the mustard seed and yeast			13:18–21	
The narrow door into the Kingdom			13:22–30	

Main Events	Matthew	Mark	Luke	John
Jesus warned by Pharisees, weeps over Jerusalem			13:31–35	
In the home of a Pharisee and parable of the banquet			14:1–24	
Counting the cost of discipleship			14:25–35	
Parables: Lost sheep, lost coin, lost son			15:1–32	
Parable: The shrewd manager; rich man and Lazarus			16:1–31	
Rebuking an erring brother; faith and duty			17:1–10	
Parable: the persistent widow			18:1–8	
Parable: the Pharisee and Tax Collector			18:9–14	
Jesus' teaching on divorce	19:1–12	10:1–12		
Receiving little children	19:13–15	10:13–16	18:15–17	
The rich young man	19:16–30	10:17–31	18:18–30	
Parable of the vineyard	20:1–16			
'Going up to Jerusalem': Jesus predicts his death	20:17–19	10:32–34	18:31–34	
The request of the mother of James and John	20:20–28	10:35–45		
'Leaving Jericho': healing two blind men (Bartimaeus)	20:29–34	10:46–52	18:35–43	
At Jericho: The conversion of Zacchaeus			19:1–10	
Parable of ten minas			19:11–27	
Bethany: In the home of Simon, Jesus anointed by Mary	26:6–13	14:1–11		12:1–11
Jerusalem (John 12:12 'The next day')				
Sunday: The triumphal entry	21:1–11	11:1–11	19:28–44	12:12–19
Monday/Tuesday:				
The fig tree withered	21:18–22	11:12–14, 20–26		
Second cleansing the temple and return to Bethany	21:12–17	11:15–19	19:45–48	
The Greeks' request and Jesus predicts his death				12:20–36
Many of the Jews will not believe, but some do				12:37–50
Jesus' authority questioned	21:23–27	11:27–33	20:1–8	
Parable of the tenants	21:33–46	12:1–12	20:9–19	
Parables: the two sons and a wedding banquet	21:28 to 22:14			

Main Events	Matthew	Mark	Luke	John
Paying taxes to Caesar	22:15–22	12:13–17	20:20–26	
Marriage and the Resurrection	22:23–33	12:18–27	20:27–39	
The greatest commandment	22:34–40	12:28–34		
Jesus explains that he is the Son of God	22:41–46	12:35–40	20:41–47	
Seven Woes	23:1–39			
The widow's offering		12:41–44	21:1–4	
Destruction of the Temple and signs of the end	24:1–51	13:1–37	17:20–37; 21:5–38	
Parables: ten virgins, talents, sheep and goats	25:1–46			
The plot against Jesus and Judas' betrayal	26:1–5, 14–16		22:1–6	
Wednesday:				
The Last Supper	26:17–30	14:12–26	22:7–38	
Jesus washed his disciples' feet				13:1–17
Jesus warns of a betrayer				13:18–30
Peter's denial predicted	26:31–35	14:27–31		13:31–38
Jesus' encouragement and promise of the Spirit				14:1–31
The vine and the branches				15:1–17
Warning of persecution				15:18 to 16:4
The ministry of the Spirit				16:5–16
Their grief will turn to joy				16:17–33
Jesus' prayer for his disciples				17:1–26
Gethsemane on the Mount of Olives	26:36–45	14:32–42	22:39–46	18:1
Jesus' betrayal and arrest	26:47–56	14:43–52	22:47–53	18:2–11
Wednesday/Thursday:				
Jesus taken before Annas				18:12–14, 19–23
Jesus before the High Priest, Caiaphas	26:57–68	14:53	22:54	
Jesus mocked and beaten and Peter's denial	26:58, 69–75	14:54–72	22:54–65	18:15–18, 25–26
Thursday:				
Jesus condemned by the Jewish Sanhedrin	27:1	15:1	22:66–71	
Judas' remorse and death	27:3–10			

Main Events	Matthew	Mark	Luke	John
Jesus before Pilate	27:2, 11–14	15:1–5	23:1–5	18:28–40
Jesus before Herod			23:6–12	
Friday:				
Jesus before Pilate again	27:15–26	15:6–15	23:13–25	19:1–16
Jesus handed over to the soldiers and beaten	27:27–31	15:16–20		
Simon of Cyrene carries the cross	27:32	15:21	23:26	
The crucifixion of Jesus (9.00 am)	27:33–44	15:22–32	23:27–38	19:17–27
The repentant thief			23:39–43	
Jesus' death (3.00 pm)	27:45–56	15:33–41	23:44–49	19:28–37
His burial by Joseph and Nicodemus	27:57–61	15:42–47	23:50–56	19:38–42
The guard at the tomb	27:62–66			
The resurrection:				
The women at the tomb	28:1–10	16:1–8	24:1–11	
Mary Magdalene and Jesus				20:1–2, 11–18
Peter and John at the tomb			24:12	20:3–10
The rumour spread by the Jews	28:11–15			
Jesus meets with Mary Magdalene		16:9–11		
Two on the Emmaus road		16:12–13	24:13–35	
Jesus meets with the ten disciples			24:36–49	20:19–23
With the eleven including Thomas		16:14		20:24–31
Breakfast by the Lake				21:1–14
Peter's profession of love				21:15–23
Jesus' commission to the disciples and his ascension	28:16–20	16:15–20	24:50–53	
(The record of the ascension in Acts 1:1–11)				
John's final confirmation of the truth of his Gospel				21:24–25

6. Where did they write their letters?

The Acts of the Apostles and where all the letters fit in.

This outline of the Acts of the Apostles can be downloaded as a PDF. Go to https://www.dayone.co.uk/collections/books/all-you-need-to-know

The formation of the church: Acts 1–12 (AD 33–46)

Luke saw the Acts as the epilogue to his Gospel. For us it is the prologue to world evangelism. The dates can only be approximate.

Acts	Date	Location	Events
1:1–11	33	Jerusalem	The final promise and the ascension of Christ.
1:12–26			Judas is replaced by Matthias.
2:1–39			Pentecost and the coming of the Holy Spirit. Peter's first sermon.
2:40–47			Those converted and the life of the early Christian community.
3:1–26			The healing of the lame man and Peter's second sermon.
4:1–22			Peter and John arrested and warned not to preach.
4:23–31			The response of the Christians in prayer.
4:32–37			A further description of the life of the Christian community.
5:1–11			The deceit and punishment of Ananias and Sapphira.
5:12–16			Signs and wonders by the apostles.
5:17–42			Peter and John imprisoned. The miraculous release and a further trial.
			The advice of Gamaliel.
6:1–7			The appointment of some to serve the community in practical matters.
6:8–7:60			The preaching and martyrdom of Stephen.
8:1–3			The Christians scattered through persecution and Saul set to destroy the church.
8:4–40		Samaria	Philip and Simon the sorcerer and the Ethiopian treasurer.
		Azotus	Philip continues itinerant evangelism.

		Caesarea	
9:1–30		Damascus	The dramatic conversion of Saul and his first evangelism.
		Caesarea	Violent opposition to Saul means that he is sent by the disciples
		Tarsus	back to his home-town of Tarsus via Caesarea.
9:31–43		Lydda	Peter visits the Christians at Lydda and heals Aeneas.
		Joppa	Peter heals Dorcas.
10:1–48		Caesarea	Peter's vision at Joppa and the conversion of the centurion Cornelius and his household.
11:1–18		Jerusalem	Peter reports to the church in Jerusalem God's work among the Gentiles.
11:19–30	45	Antioch (Syria)	As a result of Stephen's martyrdom, the gospel reaches Antioch. The apostles in Jerusalem send Barnabas to check on the church in Antioch; he goes first to Tarsus to take Saul with him. Agabus prophesies a famine across the Roman empire; the Christians at Antioch plan to send help to the Christians in Judaea. Barnabas and Saul return to Jerusalem.
12:1–19		Jerusalem	James, the brother of John, executed on Herod's orders, and Peter imprisoned. His miraculous escape.
12:19–23	44	Caesarea	Herod's arrogance and self-styled deity end with his excruciating death.
12:24–25		Antioch (Syria)	Saul and Barnabas leave Jerusalem and return to Antioch.

The expansion of the church: Acts 13–18 (AD46–52)
The first overseas mission: Paul and Barnabas from Antioch AD46

Acts	Date	Location	Events	Letters written
13:1–3	46	Antioch (Syria)	Paul and Barnabas are sent to Judaea with gifts.	
13:4–12		Seleucia	The sea-port.	
		Salamis	Sea-port and commercial centre.	
		Paphos	On Cyprus, the home of Barnabas (4:36). The Roman governor, Sergius Paulus, converted. The sorcerer Elymas. Saul renamed Paul.	
13:13		Perga	John Mark leaves Paul and Barnabas and returns to Jerusalem.	

13:14–52		Antioch (in Pisidia)	Paul preaches in the synagogue. He recounts the history of the Jews up to David and then applies the gospel.	
14:1–7		Iconium	A chief city in the Roman province of Galatia. A division among the Jews, plot to kill Paul, escape.	
14:8–20		Lystra	A cripple healed. Paul and Barnabas mistaken for gods. Timothy's home-town (16:2). Jewish opposition and Paul stoned.	
14:20–21		Derbe	And the surrounding country. Many disciples added.	
14:22–23		Antioch (in Pisidia)	Returning to home base in Syrian Antioch, appointing elders in each church.	
14:24–25		Perga		
14:26		Attalia		
14:26–28		Antioch	Paul reports to the church and stays 'a long time'.	
15:1–2	48		Jewish Christians from Jerusalem arrive with a mixture of law and gospel.	Letter to the Galatians?
15:2–29		Jerusalem	Council to deal with the false teaching.	Letter of James?
15:30–38		Antioch (in Syria)	The letter from the Jerusalem Council read. Paul and Barnabas sent on a second mission	

The second overseas mission: Paul and Silas from Antioch AD49–52

Acts	**Date**	**Location**	**Events**	**Letters written**
15:39–41			Paul and Barnabas part company: Barnabas takes John Mark	
			to Cyprus; Paul takes Silas with him on mission.	
16:1–5		Derbe and Lystra	Revisiting the churches established on the first mission. Timothy joins Paul and Silas.	
16:6–8		Phrygia and Galatia	Paul restrained by the Spirit from entering Asia and Bithynia.	
16:7–10		Troas	Paul's vision to go to Macedonia.	
16:11–12		Samothrace and Neapolis		

16:12–40		Philippi	Conversion of Lydia. When a slave girl is converted, Paul and Silas are arrested and imprisoned. The jail is opened and the jailer and his family are converted.	
17:1–9		Thessalonica	Many converted. A riot in the city. Paul and Silas escape.	
17:10–15		Berea	Silas and Timothy left behind to care for the church.	
17:16–34		Athens	Paul debates in the Areopagus with the philosophers. He refers to their unknown god. A few believe.	
18:1–18	51	Corinth	Paul stays with Aquila and Priscilla. Preaches every Sabbath in the synagogue. Silas and Timothy arrive from Berea. The proconsul Gallio dismisses accusations against Paul. This opposition from the Jews convinces Paul he must now concentrate on reaching the Gentiles (non-Jews).	1 and 2 Thessa-lonians
18:18		Cenchrea	Paul has his hair cut for a vow.	
18:19–21		Ephesus	Paul debates in the synagogue and promises to return.	
18:22		Caesarea	A brief visit by Paul.	
18:22–23		Antioch	Back home for a short while to report.	
18:24 –19:1			Apollos from Alexandria in Ephesus. Aquila and Priscilla, who have remained in the city, mentor him. Apollos then leaves for Corinth, where he powerfully debates with the Jews.	

The third overseas mission: Paul from Antioch AD 53–59

Acts	Date	Location	Events	Letters written
19:1–41	55–56	Ephesus	A slow journey through Galatia and Phrygia brings Paul to Ephesus where he stays for two or three years. The disciples of John the Baptist.	1 Corinth-ians
			Paul debates in the synagogue and the lecture hall of Tyrannus and accomplishes 'extraordinary miracles'. The Jewish 'exorcists' fail. Many converts abandon their occult practices and burn their books. A riot instigated by the silversmiths over the goddess Artemis (Diana).	

20:1–2	57	Macedonia	Preaching through the area. Thessalonica?	2 Corinth-ians
20:2–3		Greece	In Corinth for three months.	Romans
20:3–6		Philippi	Paul and Luke sail from Philippi.	
20:7–12		Troas	Paul preaches at length; Eutychus falls from the window but is healed.	
20:13–16		Assos	All these en route to Jerusalem.	
		Mitylene		
		Kios		
		Samos		
20:17–38		Miletus	Paul calls the elders from Ephesus and encourages them to stand firm in the face of false teachers and persecution. He prepares them for his own death.	
21:1–16	59	Cos	The journey to Jerusalem.	
		Rhodes		
		Patara		
		Tyre	Paul and Luke stay with the disciples for a week. An emotional farewell on the beach.	
		Ptolemais	A day with the Christians there.	
		Caesarea	Paul and Luke stay with Philip the evangelist.	
			Agabus prophesies Paul's arrest in Jerusalem. Paul's response.	

From Jerusalem to Rome

Acts	Date	Location	Events	Letters written
21:16–26	59	Jerusalem	Paul stays at the home of Mnason. Paul reports to the Christian leaders in the city. They encourage Paul to dispel the rumours that he is opposed to the Mosaic law; he undergoes a purification rite.	
21:27–40			The Jews assume Paul has taken Trophimus, a Gentile, into the temple court; a riot begins and Paul is dragged from the temple. He is rescued by the Romans.	
22:1–29			Paul's speech to the Jewish crowd. Mistakenly flogged by the Romans.	

22:30 –23:11			Paul defends himself before the Sanhedrin.	
23:12–22			The plot to assassinate Paul.	
23:23–35		Caesarea	Paul transferred to Caesarea, the headquarters of Rome in Judaea. He is held here for two years.	
24:1–27			The trial before Felix, the Roman governor.	
25:1–12			The trial before the new governor, Festus. Paul appeals to the emperor for justice.	
25:13 –26:32			The trial before Festus and Herod Agrippa.	
27:1–12	60/61		The journey to Rome. Under the charge of Julius, the centurion, and accompanied by Aristarchus from Thessalonica.	
		Sidon	Julius allows Paul to stay with his friends.	
		Myra	Here they changed ships.	
		Cnidus		
		Lasea	A sheltered bay called Fair Havens. Paul warns of the loss of the ship and cargo if they proceed further because winter is approaching. The pilot and owner overrule.	
27:13–44			The storm and shipwreck.	
28:1–10		Malta	The hospitality of the islanders. Paul invited to stay with Publius. Publius' father healed.	
28:11–16		Syracuse	They stay here for three days here on the final journey to Rome.	
		Rhegium		
		Puteoli	Paul and Luke stay a week with Christians here.	
		Forum of Appius	Brethren from Rome come to meet Paul. The Three Taverns.	
28:17–28	62	Rome	Paul's speech to the Jewish leaders in Rome.	
28:30–31			Paul spends two years under house arrest preaching and teaching.	Paul writes letters from prison: Ephesians, Colossians, Philemon, Philippians

	62?		After those two years it is thought that Paul was released and continued his mission work, possibly visiting Spain, which he had wanted to do (Romans 15:24).	1 Timothy and Titus
	67?		Paul was rearrested and martyred on the orders of the emperor Nero. The second letter to Timothy was written when Paul anticipated his imminent death.	2 Timothy

For the authorship and date of the following letters, see Book 3 chapter 6 in this series.

There is debate around the authorship of **Hebrews** since no name is attached. However, the earliest tradition (from Clement in AD 95) is that Paul was the author; there is no conclusive reason to dispute this. If it is from Paul, it was most likely written prior to AD 64.

The **two letters of Peter** were almost certainly written sometime prior to AD 64.

According to Josephus, the first century Jewish historian, **James**, the author of the New Testament letter and brother of Jesus, was martyred in AD 62. If so, the letter must pre-date this.

Dating of the letter of **Jude**, another brother of Jesus, is uncertain, although it is likely to have been sometime prior to AD 70.

The **three letters from John** were most likely written after the death of Paul and Peter, who were almost certainly martyred during the reign of Nero. If John was exiled to Patmos under the emperor Diocletian (AD 81–96), the book of **Revelation** must have been written sometime after the year 81.

7. Reading the Bible from cover to cover

This reading programme can be downloaded as a PDF. Go to https://www.dayone.co.uk/collections/books/all-you-need-to-know

Few things are more important for the Christian, or for anyone, than to read regularly the word of God—all of it: the hard, the tedious, and the mysterious, as well as the encouraging and exciting parts. There are many fine commentaries and daily reading notes, but it is essential that we know our Bible, and the only way to achieve this is by reading it through—over and over again.

The following plan ensures that in nineteen months we will have read every word of the Bible once and parts of the New Testament twice. For each day, a longer Old Testament portion is followed by a shorter New Testament reading. The brief introductions are not commentaries but simply set the reading in its context. It is vital that Christians should know the history of their faith and how each book of the Bible fits into the unfolding of God's promise and plans.

The titles of the psalms are not necessarily part of the inerrant Scriptures, but they do indicate the occasion for some of them. Here, the psalms are placed either according to the title or where their theme seems most appropriate. The reader should always take note of the psalm title.

For those who are not familiar with the history of the biblical narrative, it will be helpful to follow the outline of the Old Testament (chapter 4) and the outline of the Acts of the Apostles (chapter 6) in conjunction with the daily reading.

Genesis means 'beginning'. It begins with the account of how God created the universe and life in all its forms. This first book in the Bible introduces us to the human race and its development, marriage, sexuality, sin, salvation and the chosen people, language, government, culture, nations, geography, religion, and much more. There is no such thing as pre-history because there is no history before God's record in Genesis. This is God's revelation of origins. From the time of Noah and the global flood, our focus shifts to the family and descendants of Abraham and God's promise of a chosen people that will eventually lead to the Saviour, Jesus Christ.		**Matthew** was a disciple of Christ and his Gospel focuses on Christ as King. His genealogy of Jesus is traced back to Adam through the line of Joseph, who was the legal father of Jesus.	
1.	Genesis 1–2	1.	Matthew 1
2.	Psalms 19; 104	2.	Matthew 2:1–18
3.	Genesis 3–4	3.	Matthew 2:19–3:12
4.	Genesis 5–7:5	4.	Matthew 3:13–4:17
5.	Genesis 7:6–8:22	5.	Matthew 4:18–5:12
6.	Genesis 9; Psalm 29	6.	Matthew 5:13–26
7	Genesis 10–11:26	7.	Matthew 5:27–47
8.	Genesis 11:27–13	8.	Matthew 6:1–18
9.	Genesis 14–15	9.	Matthew 6:19–34
10	Genesis 16–17	10.	Matthew 7:1–14
11.	Genesis 18–19	11.	Matthew 7:15–29
12	Genesis 20–21	12.	Matthew 8:1–17
13	Genesis 22–23	13.	Matthew 8:18–34
14.	Genesis 24	14.	Matthew 9:1–17
15	Genesis 25–26	15.	Matthew 9:18–38
16.	Genesis 27–28:9	16.	Matthew 10:1–25
17.	Genesis 28:10–30:24	17.	Matthew 10:26–42
18.	Genesis 30:25–31:35	18.	Matthew 11:1–19
19.	Genesis 31:36–32:21	19.	Matthew 11:20–30
20.	Genesis 32:22–34	20.	Matthew 12:1–21
21.	Genesis 35–36	21.	Matthew 12:22–37
22.	Genesis 37	22.	Matthew 12:38–50
23.	Genesis 38–39	23.	Matthew 13:1–23
24	Genesis 40–41:36	24.	Matthew 13:24–43
25.	Genesis 41:37–42	25.	Matthew 13:44–58
26	Genesis 43–44:13	26.	Matthew 14:1–21

27. Genesis 44:14–45	27. Matthew 14:22–36
28. Genesis 46–47	28. Matthew 15:1–20
29. Genesis 48–49:28	29. Matthew 15:21–39
30. Genesis 49:29–Exodus 1:22	30. Matthew 16:1–20
Exodus: The account of Moses' birth, around 1526 BC, prepares for the Israelites' miraculous escape from Egypt, their early journeying through the wilderness, the giving of the law of God, and the establishing of the priesthood and tabernacle. All this is the 'shadow' of the ultimate fulfilment of God's promise in Jesus Christ (Heb. 8:5; 10:1).	
31. Exodus 2–3	31. Matthew 16:21–28
32. Exodus 4–5:21	32. Matthew 17:1–13
33. Exodus 5:22–7:25	33. Matthew 17:14–27
34. Exodus 8–9:12	34. Matthew 18:1–14
35 Exodus 9:13–10:29	35. Matthew 18:15–35
36 Exodus 11–12:30	36. Matthew 19:1–15
37. Exodus 12:31–13:22	37. Matthew 19:16–30
38. Exodus 14–15:18	38. Matthew 20:1–16
39. Exodus 15:19–16:36	39. Matthew 20:17–34
40. Exodus 17–18	40. Matthew 21:1–17
Psalm 105 traces the history of Israel from Egypt into the wilderness.	
41. Psalm 105	41. Matthew 21:18–32
42. Exodus 19–20	42. Matthew 21:33–46
43 Exodus 21–22:15	43. Matthew 22:1–22
44. Exodus 22:16–23	44. Matthew 22:23–46
45. Exodus 24–25:30	45. Matthew 23:1–24
46. Exodus 25:31–26:37	46. Matthew 23:25–39
47. Exodus 27–28	47. Matthew 24:1–28
48. Exodus 29–30:10	48. Matthew 24:29–41
49. Exodus 30:11–31:18	49. Matthew 24:42–51
50. Exodus 32–33:6	50. Matthew 25:1–13
51. Exodus 33:7–34:28	51. Matthew 25:14–30
52. Exodus 34:29–36:1	52. Matthew 25:31–46
53 Exodus 36:2–37:24	53. Matthew 26:1–16
54. Exodus 37:25–39:21	54. Matthew 26:17–35
55. Exodus 39:22–40:38	55. Matthew 26:36–56

Leviticus is the book of instructions for the priests from the tribe of Levi and those from the line of Aaron. All the ceremonial details prefigure the once-for-all sacrifice of Christ.	
56. Leviticus 1–3	56. Matthew 26:57–68
57. Leviticus 4–5:13	57. Matthew 26:69–27:10
58. Leviticus 5:14–7:27	58. Matthew 27:11–26
59. Leviticus 7:28–8:36	59. Matthew 27:27–44
60. Leviticus 9–10	60. Matthew 27:45–61
61. Leviticus 11–12	61. Matthew 27:62–28
	Acts is the thrilling narrative of the young church in action from the ascension of Christ to a little beyond the middle of the first century. We will read Acts through twice, and on this first occasion we read it straight through without digressing to read the letters Paul wrote throughout his mission journeys.
62. Leviticus 13	62. Acts 1:1–11
63. Leviticus 14	63. Acts 1:12–26
64. Leviticus 15	64. Acts 2:1–13
65. Leviticus 16	65. Acts 2:14–28
66. Leviticus 17–18	66. Acts 2:29–41
67. Leviticus 19–20	67. Acts 2:42–3:10
68. Leviticus 21–22	68. Acts 3:11–26
69. Leviticus 23	69. Acts 4:1–22
70. Leviticus 24–25:34	70. Acts 4:23–37
71. Leviticus 25:35–26:13	71. Acts 5:1–16
72. Leviticus 26:14–27:34	72. Acts 5:17–28
In addition to giving a detailed census of the people who left Egypt, **Numbers** continues the account of the epic wilderness journey.	
73. Numbers 1	73. Acts 5:29–42
74. Numbers 2–3:26	74. Acts 6
75. Numbers 3:27–4:28	75. Acts 7:1–16
76. Numbers 4:29–5:31	76. Acts 7:17–34
77. Numbers 6–7:35	77. Acts 7:35–53
78. Numbers 7:36–8:4	78. Acts 7:54–8:8
79. Numbers 8:5–9:23	79. Acts 8:9–25
80. Numbers 10–11:15	80. Acts 8:26–40
81. Numbers 11:16–12:16	81. Acts 9:1–19
82. Numbers 13–14:25	82. Acts 9:20–31

83. Numbers 14:26–15:41	83. Acts 9:32–43
84. Numbers 16–17	84. Acts 10:1–23
85. Numbers 18–19	85. Acts 10:24–48
86. Numbers 20–21:20	86. Acts 11:1–18
87. Numbers 21:21–22:41	87. Acts 11:19–30
88. Numbers 23–24	88. Acts 12:1–17
89. Numbers 25–26:51	89. Acts 12:18–25
90. Numbers 26:52–28:15	90. Acts 13:1–12
91. Numbers 28:16–29:40	91. Acts 13:13–31
92. Numbers 30–31	92. Acts 13:32–52
93. Numbers 32	93. Acts 14:1–18
94. Numbers 33–34:9	94. Acts 14:19–28
95. Numbers 34:10–36:13	95. Acts 15:1–21
Deuteronomy means 'the second law': it revisits and expands on the giving of the law recorded in Exodus. After more details of the wilderness journey we are brought to the death of Moses.	
96. Deuteronomy 1	96. Acts 15:22–35
97. Deuteronomy 2–3:11	97. Acts 15:36–16:15
98. Deuteronomy 3:12–4:20	98. Acts 16:16–40
99. Deuteronomy 4:21–5:33	99. Acts 17:1–15
100. Deuteronomy 6–7	100. Acts 17:16–34
101. Deuteronomy 8–9	101. Acts 18:1–17
102. Deuteronomy 10–11:21	102. Acts 18:18–28
103. Deuteronomy 11:22–12:32	103. Acts 19:1–20
104. Deuteronomy 13–14	104. Acts 19:21–41
105. Deuteronomy 15–16	105. Acts 20:1–16
106. Deuteronomy 17–19	106. Acts 20:17–38
107. Deuteronomy 20–22	107. Acts 21:1–16
108. Deuteronomy 23–24	108. Acts 21:17–26
109. Deuteronomy 25–26	109. Acts 21:27–39
110. Deuteronomy 27–28:44	110. Acts 21:40–22:21
111. Deuteronomy 28:45–29:29	111. Acts 22:22–29
112. Deuteronomy 30–31:29	112. Acts 22:30–23:11
113. Deuteronomy 31:30–32:52	113. Acts 23:12–22
114. Deuteronomy 33–34	114. Acts 23:23–35
The first of these **psalms** belongs to Moses himself; the rest are anonymous but are appropriate to this period.	
115. Psalms 90–91	115. Acts 24
116. Psalms 92–94	116. Acts 25:1–12

117. Psalms 95–97	117. Acts 25:13–27
118. Psalms 98–100	118. Acts 26:1–18
Moses' appointed successor, **Joshua**, leads the Israelites across the Jordan and into the Promised Land, and divides the land among the twelve tribes.	
119. Joshua 1–2	119. Acts 26:19–32
120. Joshua 3–4	120. Acts 27:1–12
121. Joshua 5–6	121. Acts 27:13–26
122. Joshua 7–8:29	122. Acts 27:27–44
123. Joshua 8:30–10:15	123. Acts 28
	John was one of the disciples of Christ and the writer of three letters that bear his name as well as the book of Revelation. John does not relate the birth or the parables of Christ, presumably because he knew that Matthew and Luke had adequately covered those areas. He deliberately adds some of the miracles and prayers of Jesus that are not mentioned by the others. Half of John's Gospel is devoted to the last week in the life of Jesus.
124. Joshua 10:16–11:23	124. John 1:1–18
125. Joshua 12–13	125. John 1:19–34
126. Joshua 14–15	126. John 1:35–51
127. Joshua 16–18:10	127. John 2:1–12
128. Joshua 18:11–19:51	128. John 2:13–25
129. Joshua 20–22:9	129. John 3:1–21
130. Joshua 22:10–34	130. John 3:22–36
131. Joshua 23–24	131. John 4:1–26
Joshua died around the year 1356 BC at the age of 110. During the three hundred years that followed, Israel was occasionally led by fifteen '**judges**', including Eli and Samuel. It was a period of virtual anarchy, with the tragic downward spiral of apostasy (when the people abandoned God for the idols around them), oppression (through one of the surrounding tribal nations sent by God in judgement), repentance (by Israel as they cried for help), deliverance (by a judge chosen by God)—and the cycle was repeated over again.	

132. Judges 1–2	132. John 4:27–54
133. Judges 3–4:10	133. John 5:1–18
134. Judges 4:11–5:31	134. John 5:19–29
135. Judges 6–7:8	135. John 5:30–47
136. Judges 7:9–8:35	136. John 6:1–21
137. Judges 9	137. John 6:22–40
138. Judges 10–11	138. John 6:41–71
139. Judges 12–13	139. John 7:1–24
140. Judges 14–15	140. John 7:25–44
141. Judges 16	141. John 7:45–8:11
142. Judges 17–18	142. John 8:12–30
143. Judges 19–20:18	143. John 8:31–47
144. Judges 20:19–21:25	144. John 8:48–59
These two **psalms** review the escape from Egypt, the entry into the Promised Land and the unfaithfulness of Israel to their faithful God.	
145. Psalm 106	145. John 9:1–12
146. Psalm 107	146. John 9:13–25
In the midst of the mayhem and misery of the period of the judges, the story of **Ruth** and Boaz reveals God guarding his chosen line, leading to David and the Messiah, Jesus.	
147. Ruth 1–2	147. John 9:26–41
148. Ruth 3–4	148. John 10:1–21
Samuel is the last of the judges and the account now prepares for the monarchy, when the people demand a king in order to be like the surrounding nations.	
149. 1 Samuel 1–2:11	149. John 10:22–42
150. 1 Samuel 2:12–3:21	150. John 11:1–16
151. 1 Samuel 4–5	151. John 11:17–37
152. 1 Samuel 6–7	152. John 11:38–57
153. 1 Samuel 8–9:21	153. John 12:1–11
154. 1 Samuel 9:22–11:15	154. John 12:12–26
155. 1 Samuel 12–13:15	155. John 12:27–36
156. 1 Samuel 13:16–14:48	156. John 12:37–50
157. 1 Samuel 14:49–15:35	157. John 13:1–20
158. 1 Samuel 16–17	158. John 13:21–30
159. 1 Samuel 18–19	159. John 13:31–14:4

Psalm 59 is from David after Saul had sent men to arrest him at his home. The following **psalms**, interwoven into David's life story, reveal his heart for God at all times. The titles to the psalms indicate the occasions for some of them.	
160. Psalm 59	160. John 14:5–14
161. Psalms 1–5	161. John 14:15–31
162. Psalms 6–10	162. John 15:1–17
163. 1 Samuel 20	163. John 15:18–16:4
164. 1 Samuel 21; Psalms 52; 34; 56	164. John 16:5–15
165. 1 Samuel 22–23:6	165. John 16:16–33
166. Psalms 57; 58; 53	166. John 17:1–12
167. 1 Samuel 23:7–24; Psalms 54; 55	167. John 17:13–26
168. 1 Samuel 25	168. John 18:1–14
169. 1 Samuel 26; Psalm 18	169. John 18:15–27
170. Psalms 138–139	170. John 18:28–40
171. Psalms 140–142	171. John 19:1–16
172. Psalms 143–145	172. John 19:17–27
173. 1 Samuel 27	173. John 19:28–42
174. 1 Samuel 28–29	174. John 20:1–18
175. 1 Samuel 30–31	175. John 20:19–31
176. Psalms 42–44	176. John 21:1–14
177. Psalms 45–47	177. John 21:15–25
	The identity of the author of the letter to the **Hebrews** has long been disputed. However, the best and oldest tradition is that it belongs to Paul, and the closing verses imply that it was written from Rome during Paul's house arrest there. It was written primarily to Jewish Christians, encouraging them to appreciate the vast difference between their old way of legal and ceremonial requirements and the freedom of faith in Christ. There are magnificent descriptions of the nature of Christ and his sacrifice.
178. Psalms 48–50	178. Hebrews 1:1–9
179. 2 Samuel 1–2:7	179. Hebrews 1:10–2:4
180. 2 Samuel 2:8–3:21	180. Hebrews 2:5–18
181. 2 Samuel 3:22–5:16	181. Hebrews 3
182. 2 Samuel 5:17–6:23	182. Hebrews 4:1–13

183. Psalms 65–67	183. Hebrews 4:14–5:10
184. Psalm 68	184. Hebrews 5:11–6:12
185. 2 Samuel 7	185. Hebrews 6:13–7:10
186. 2 Samuel 8–10	186. Hebrews 7:11–28
187. Psalms 60–62	187. Hebrews 8
188. 2 Samuel 11–12	188. Hebrews 9:1–10
189. Psalm 51	189. Hebrews 9:11–28
190. 2 Samuel 13	190. Hebrews 10:1–18
191. 2 Samuel 14	191. Hebrews 10:19–39
192. 2 Samuel 15–16:14	192. Hebrews 11:1–12
193. 2 Samuel 16:15–17:29	193. Hebrews 11:13–28
194. Psalms 1–4	194. Hebrews 11:29–12:2
195. Psalms 63–64; 69	195. Hebrews 12:3–17
196. Psalms 70; 71	196. Hebrews 12:18–29
197. 2 Samuel 18–19:8	197. Hebrews 13:1–14
198. 2 Samuel 19:9–20:26	198. Hebrews 13:15–25
	Luke may not have been an eyewitness to all the details of the life of Christ, but he had access to many reliable sources, and he promises a careful and orderly account of the birth, ministry, death and resurrection of Christ. Luke, a doctor by profession, was also the writer of the Acts of the Apostles and a companion of Paul on many of Paul's travels.
199. 2 Samuel 21–22:51	199. Luke 1:1–25
200. 2 Samuel 23–24	200. Luke 1:26–45
201. Psalms 11–13	201. Luke 1:46–66
202. Psalms 14–16	202. Luke 1:67–80
203. Psalms 20–22	203. Luke 2:1–20
204. Psalms 23–25	204. Luke 2:21–35
205. Psalms 26–28	205. Luke 2:36–52
206. Psalms 30–31	206. Luke 3:1–20
207. Psalms 32–33	207. Luke 3:21–38
208. Psalms 35–36	208. Luke 4:1–21
209. Psalm 37	209. Luke 4:22–37
210. Psalms 38–39	210. Luke 4:38–5:11
211. Psalms 40–41	211. Luke 5:12–26
Kings: Nearing the end of his life, David prepared Solomon to be his successor, overlooking Adonijah, who was the first in line to the throne.	

212. 1 Kings 1	212. Luke 5:27–39
213. 1 Kings 2	213. Luke 6:1–16
214. 1 Kings 3–4:28	214. Luke 6:17–36
215. 1 Kings 4:29–34; Psalm 72	215. Luke 6:37–49
216. 1 Kings 5–6	216. Luke 7:1–17
217. 1 Kings 7	217. Luke 7:18–35
218. 1 Kings 8:1–53	218. Luke 7:36–50
219. 1 Kings 8:54–9:28	219. Luke 8:1–15
220. 1 Kings 10	220. Luke 8:16–25
221. 1 Kings 11	221. Luke 8: 26–39
Solomon is still known for his outstanding spiritual and moral wisdom, which is reflected in these **proverbs**. The final two chapters come from different and unknown hands, and the queen mother of Lemuel closes with a beautiful description of an exemplary wife.	
222. Proverbs 1	222. Luke 8:40–56
223. Proverbs 2–3	223. Luke 9:1–17
224. Proverbs 4–5	224. Luke 9:18–36
225. Proverbs 6–7	225. Luke 9:37–50
226. Proverbs 8–9	226. Luke 9:51–10:12
227. Proverbs 10	227. Luke 10:13–24
228. Proverbs 11	228. Luke 10:25–37
229. Proverbs 12–13:7	229. Luke 10:38–11:13
230. Proverbs 13:8–14:22	230. Luke 11:14–28
231. Proverbs 14:23–15:26	231. Luke 11:29–41
232. Proverbs 15:27–16:33	232. Luke 11:42–54
233. Proverbs 17–18:13	233. Luke 12:1–12
234. Proverbs 18:14–19:29	234. Luke 12:13–34
235. Proverbs 20–21:11	235. Luke 12:35–48
236. Proverbs 21:12–22:16	236. Luke 12:49–59
237. Proverbs 22:17–23:35	237. Luke 13:1–17
238. Proverbs 24–25:10	238. Luke 13:18–35
239. Proverbs 25:11–26	239. Luke 14:1–24
240. Proverbs 27–28:8	240. Luke 14:25–15:10
241. Proverbs 28:9–29:11	241. Luke 15:11–32
242. Proverbs 29:12–30:20	242. Luke 16:1–18
243. Proverbs 30:21–31:31	243. Luke 16:19–31

The traditional view of Solomon as the author of this book, mainly because of 1:1, 12, has been challenged. Some conservative scholars place it at the time of the Persian exile, over four hundred years after Solomon, and by an unknown sage who describes the meaningless of life when we leave God out and who impersonated Solomon only as a literary device. The best translation of the word '**Ecclesiastes**' is simply 'The Preacher'.	
244. Ecclesiastes 1–2	244. Luke 17:1–19
245. Ecclesiastes 3–4	245. Luke 17:20–37
246. Ecclesiastes 5–7:18	246. Luke 18:1–17
247. Ecclesiastes 7:19–9:18	247. Luke 18:18–34
248. Ecclesiastes 10–12	248. Luke 18:35–19:10
Song of Songs: This book claims Solomon as the author. It is a beautiful poem of true and pure love, but also an allegory of Christ and his bride, the church.	
249. Song of Songs 1–2	249. Luke 19:11–27
250. Song of Songs 3–5	250. Luke 19:28–48
251. Song of Songs 6–8	251. Luke 20:1–19
1–2 Kings: Solomon's final years were a disappointment as he allowed his pagan foreign wives to turn his heart and mind away from God. As a result, the kingdom that had enjoyed so much peace and stability began to fragment, as we saw in 1 Kings 11. The succession of Rehoboam saw the division of the land into ten northern tribes (Israel) based around Samaria and two southern tribes (Judah) centred upon Jerusalem.	
252. 1 Kings 12	252. Luke 20:20–40
253. 1 Kings 13:1–14:20	253. Luke 20:41–21:19
254. 1 Kings 14:21–16:7	254. Luke 21:20–38
255. 1 Kings 16:8–17:24	255. Luke 22:1–23
256. 1 Kings 18	256. Luke 22:24–38
257. 1 Kings 19–20:25	257. Luke 22:39–62
258. 1 Kings 20:26–21:29	258. Luke 22:63–23:12
259. 1 Kings 22	259. Luke 23:13–31

260. 2 Kings 1–2:18	260. Luke 23:32–49
261. 2 Kings 2:19–3:27	261. Luke 23:50–24:12
262. 2 Kings 4	262. Luke 24:13–35
263. 2 Kings 5:1–6:7	263. Luke 24:36–53
	This is our second reading of **Acts**, and this time we will stop off to read the letters of Paul where they fit into the narrative. This will appear a little disjointed but will enable us to appreciate that Paul's letters were written into the living context of active churches.
264. 2 Kings 6:8–7:20	264. Acts 1:1–11
Obadiah is probably the earliest of our 'minor prophets', preaching in the time of Jehoram, king of Judah, around 846 BC. He warns Edom for its cruelty and reminds them that salvation is found only in Judah.	
265. 2 Kings 8:1–24; Obadiah	265. Acts 1:12–26
266. 2 Kings 8:25–9:13	266. Acts 2:1–13
267. 2 Kings 9:14–10:17	267. Acts 2:14–28
268. 2 Kings 10:18–11:21	268. Acts 2:29–41
269. 2 Kings 12–13:9	269. Acts 2:42–3:10
270. 2 Kings 13:10–14:25	270. Acts 3:11–26
Apart from his own account of his eventual preaching at Nineveh, the capital of the powerful and cruel Assyrian empire, **Jonah** is only mentioned in 2 Kings 14:25, which places him at the time of Jeroboam of Israel, sometime after 782 BC.	
271. Jonah 1–2	271. Acts 4:1–22
272. Jonah 3–4	272. Acts 4:23–37
A century and a half after Jonah, **Nahum** warned the mighty Assyrian Empire of their approaching demise. Thebes (in Egypt) has already fallen (3:8–10), so this dates Nahum after 663 BC. His prophecies against Nineveh were fulfilled in detail in 612 BC, when the Babylonians destroyed the great city.	
273. Nahum 1–3	273. Acts 5:1–16
274. 2 Kings 14:26–15:38	274. Acts 5:17–28
275. 2 Kings 16–17	275. Acts 5:29–42

276. 2 Kings 18	276. Acts 6
277. 2 Kings 19	277. Acts 7:1–16
278. 2 Kings 20–21:18	278. Acts 7:17–34
279. 2 Kings 21:19–23:14	279. Acts 7:35–53
280. 2 Kings 23:15–24:7	280. Acts 7:54–8:8
281. 2 Kings 24:8–25:30	281. Acts 8:9–25
The first of these three **psalms** was evidently written when the Jews were led into their Babylonian captivity in 587 BC. The second reflects their return to Jerusalem after the decree of Cyrus in 539 BC.	
282. Psalms 137, 126, 146	282. Acts 8:26–40
Jeremiah was the prophet in Jerusalem from the reign of Josiah to the destruction of Jerusalem in the time of Zedekiah and the subsequent Babylonian exile in 587 BC. His warning of the impending judgement on the city made Jeremiah the most hated man in Judah.	
283. Jeremiah 1–2:13	283. Acts 9:1–19
284. Jeremiah 2:14–37	284. Acts 9:20–31
285. Jeremiah 3	285. Acts 9:32–43
286. Jeremiah 4	286. Acts 10:1–23
287. Jeremiah 5	287. Acts 10:24–48
288. Jeremiah 6	288. Acts 11:1–18
289. Jeremiah 7	289. Acts 11:19–30
290. Jeremiah 8	290. Acts 12:1–18
291. Jeremiah 9	291. Acts 12:19–25
292. Jeremiah 10	292. Acts 13:1–12
293. Jeremiah 11	293. Acts 13:13–31
294. Jeremiah 12	294. Acts 13:32–52
295. Jeremiah 13	295. Acts 14:1–18
296. Jeremiah 14	296. Acts 14:19–28
297. Jeremiah 15	297. Acts 15:1–21

	The Council at Jerusalem was vital for the gospel. Jewish converts arrived from Jerusalem claiming that the Gentiles must conform to aspects of the law given through Moses. It was a message of justification by faith and ceremonial works. **Galatians** may be the earliest letter of Paul on record, written around AD 48 (either just before or after the Council), to the Christians in Galatia who were adopting the heresy of the 'Judaizers'. It contains Paul's personal testimony, a warning against the false gospel, and a reminder of the freedom there is in Christ. Apart from the usual cluster of critics, there has never been serious doubt about the authorship of the thirteen letters (not counting Hebrews) that have Paul's name on them. They are all included in the earliest lists of the Christian canon of the New Testament books.
298. Jeremiah 16:1–17:8	298. Galatians 1
299. Jeremiah 17:9–18:17	299. Galatians 2:1–10
300. Jeremiah 18:18–19:15	300. Galatians 2:11–21
301. Jeremiah 20–21	301. Galatians 3:1–14
302. Jeremiah 22	302. Galatians 3:15–29
303. Jeremiah 23:1–24	303. Galatians 4:1–20
304. Jeremiah 23:25–25:14	304. Galatians 4:21–31
305. Jeremiah 25:15–26:9	305. Galatians 5
306. Jeremiah 26:10–27:22	306. Galatians 6
	It is generally accepted that the author of the letter of **James** was one of the brothers of Jesus and the acknowledged wise spokesman in Acts 15:13, and therefore not the apostle who was killed by Herod (Acts 12:2) shortly before Herod's death in AD 44. The Jewish historian Josephus records that James the brother of Jesus was martyred around AD 62. The letter of James, probably sent before the Council at Jerusalem, deals with practical Christian living and reminds the readers that our faith can only be seen by the quality of the life we live.

307. Jeremiah 28–29:14	307. James 1:1–18
308. Jeremiah 29:15–30:11	308. James 1:19–27
309. Jeremiah 30:12–31:14	309. James 2:1–13
310. Jeremiah 31:15–40	310. James 2:14–26
311. Jeremiah 32:1–35	311. James 3
312. Jeremiah 32:36–33:26	312. James 4
313. Jeremiah 34–35	313. James 5
	Paul and his companions embark on their first evangelistic mission across Asia Minor (modern-day Turkey).
314. Jeremiah 36	314. Acts 15:22–35
315. Jeremiah 37–38:13	315. Acts 15:36–16:15
316. Jeremiah 38:14–39:18	316. Acts 16:16–40
317. Jeremiah 40–41	317. Acts 17:1–15
318. Jeremiah 42–43	318. Acts 17:16–34
319. Jeremiah 44	319. Acts 18:1–17
	During his stay in Corinth, Paul was arraigned before the proconsul Gallio, whom we know was in office in AD 51/52. This fixes the date of Paul's letters to the **Thessalonians**. Timothy arrived with good news of the healthy church there in Macedonia and Paul wrote to commend and encourage them; he also responded to their query about what happens when believers die.
320. Jeremiah 45–46	320. 1 Thessalonians 1–2:12
321. Jeremiah 47–48:20	321. 1 Thessalonians 2:13–20
322. Jeremiah 48:21–47	322. 1 Thessalonians 3
323. Jeremiah 49:1–22	323. 1 Thessalonians 4
324. Jeremiah 49:23–50:7	324. 1 Thessalonians 5
	A few months later, while still in Corinth, Paul wrote again to correct a misunderstanding from his first letter and outlined signs of the end times. There are final instructions to pray and work.
325. Jeremiah 50:8–24	325. 2 Thessalonians 1
326. Jeremiah 50:25–46	326. 2 Thessalonians 2
327. Jeremiah 51:1–23	327. 2 Thessalonians 3

	After a brief return to home base in Antioch, Paul set out on his third mission and arrived in Ephesus, where he spent two years from AD 55 to 57.
328. Jeremiah 51:24–44	328. Acts 18:18–28
329. Jeremiah 51:45–64	329. Acts 19:1–20
330. Jeremiah 52	330. Acts 19:21–41
As the title indicates, this is a **lament** of Jeremiah over the destruction of Jerusalem, something he had been prophesying for many years. However, there is hope for the remnant.	Paul's relationship with the church in Corinth in Greece was never easy. He had written a 'previous letter' to warn them not to associate with immoral people, which was apparently misunderstood (5:9–11). Meanwhile, during his time in Ephesus, Paul heard of moral disorders and disunity within the church and wrote this strong corrective in **1 Corinthians**—which was also resented as interference. Here he also deals with the subjects of the Lord's Supper, spiritual gifts and the resurrection.
331. Lamentations 1	331. 1 Corinthians 1:1–17
332. Lamentations 2	332. 1 Corinthians 1:18–31
333. Lamentations 3	333. 1 Corinthians 2
334. Lamentations 4–5	334. 1 Corinthians 3
Ezekiel was taken into captivity to Babylon with Jehoiachin in 597 BC and from there warns Jerusalem of its final destruction, which came in 587 BC. He also warns the surrounding nations of their own judgement for mocking Judah. The later chapters are symbolic of the kingdom of God.	
335. Ezekiel 1–2	335. 1 Corinthians 4
336. Ezekiel 3–4	336. 1 Corinthians 5
337. Ezekiel 5–6	337. 1 Corinthians 6
338. Ezekiel 7–8	338. 1 Corinthians 7:1–24
339. Ezekiel 9–10	339. 1 Corinthians 7:25–40
340. Ezekiel 11–12:16	340. 1 Corinthians 8
341. Ezekiel 12:17–13	341. 1 Corinthians 9:1–18
342. Ezekiel 14–15	342. 1 Corinthians 9:19–10:13
343. Ezekiel 16:1–34	343. 1 Corinthians 10:14–11:1
344. Ezekiel 16:35–63	344. 1 Corinthians 11:2–16
345. Ezekiel 17–18:9	345. 1 Corinthians 11:17–34
346. Ezekiel 18:10–19:14	346. 1 Corinthians 12:1–13

347. Ezekiel 20:1–29	347. 1 Corinthians 12:14–31
348. Ezekiel 20:30–21:17	348. 1 Corinthians 13
349. Ezekiel 21:18–22:22	349. 1 Corinthians 14:1–12
350. Ezekiel 22:23–23:27	350. 1 Corinthians 14:13–25
351. Ezekiel 23:28–24:14	351. 1 Corinthians 14:26–40
352. Ezekiel 24:15–25:7	352. 1 Corinthians 15:1–19
353. Ezekiel 26:1–27:11	353. 1 Corinthians 15:20–34
354. Ezekiel 27:12–36	354. 1 Corinthians 15:35–58
355. Ezekiel 28	355. 1 Corinthians 16
	Paul made what he described as a 'painful visit' to Corinth (2 Cor. 2:1) and wrote again 'out of great distress and anguish of heart' (2:4). At Troas Paul expected news from Corinth through Titus, but hearing nothing and having 'no peace of mind', he moved back to Thessalonica (in Macedonia), where Titus arrived with good news of the repentance of the church in Corinth. Paul immediately sent off 2 Corinthians expressing his hope to visit them soon; this visit is probably recorded in Acts 20:2–3. Paul travelled from Ephesus through Macedonia (Thessalonica), Greece (Corinth), Troas, and on to Miletus.
356. Ezekiel 29–30:9	356. Acts 20:1–16
357. Ezekiel 30:10–31:18	357. Acts 20:17–38
	2 Corinthians, which, as we have seen, may have been his fourth letter to them, expressed his joy at their change of mind and advised them on, among other issues, how to deal with a repentant member. In this letter Paul established his own apostolic credentials and warned against false apostles. Written from Macedonia around AD 58, this letter expresses Paul's hope to visit them soon for the third time.
358. Ezekiel 32	358. 2 Corinthians 1:1–11
359. Ezekiel 33	359. 2 Corinthians 1:12–2:4
360. Ezekiel 34	360. 2 Corinthians 2:5–17
361. Ezekiel 35–36:21	361. 2 Corinthians 3
362. Ezekiel 36:22–37:28	362. 2 Corinthians 4
363. Ezekiel 38–39:10	363. 2 Corinthians 5

364. Ezekiel 39:11–40:19	364. 2 Corinthians 6–7:1
365. Ezekiel 40:20–49	365. 2 Corinthians 7:2–16
366. Ezekiel 41–42	366. 2 Corinthians 8:1–15
367. Ezekiel 43–44	367. 2 Corinthians 8:16–9:5
368. Ezekiel 45–46	368. 2 Corinthians 9:6–15
369. Ezekiel 47–48	369. 2 Corinthians 10
Daniel was a contemporary of Ezekiel and went into exile at about the same time. The book does not follow a strictly chronological order—chapters 7 and 8 immediately precede chapter 5 chronologically. Daniel held office under at least five pagan despots. Nothing negative is ever written of Daniel in the Bible.	
370. Daniel 1–2:13	370. 2 Corinthians 11:1–15
371. Daniel 2:14–49	371. 2 Corinthians 11:16–33
372. Daniel 3	372. 2 Corinthians 12:1–10
373. Daniel 4	373. 2 Corinthians 12:11–21
374. Daniel 5	374. 2 Corinthians 13
	All the evidence points to the fact that Paul wrote the letter to the church at **Rome** during his three months' stay in Corinth in AD 58 (Acts 20:2–3); it was taken to Rome by Phoebe, a member of the church in Corinth. The church met at the home of Gaius, who we know lived in Corinth; we also know from inscriptions that Erastus was a local government officer in Corinth at this time (Rom. 16:23; see also 2 Tim. 4:20). This is the most valuable and concise book of Christian doctrine in the Bible. It deals with the origin of the human race, sin and its results, justification by faith alone, the new life in Christ, predestination, God's plan for Israel, practical Christian living, and more. It concludes with personal greetings.
375. Daniel 6	375. Romans 1:1–17
376. Daniel 7	376. Romans 1:18–32
377. Daniel 8	377. Romans 2:1–16
378. Daniel 9	378. Romans 2:17–29
379. Daniel 10:1–11:13	379. Romans 3:1–20

380. Daniel 11:14–45	380. Romans 3:21–4:8
381. Daniel 12	381. Romans 4:9–25
Chronicles covers much of the ground we have already read in Kings; sometimes the text is identical and elsewhere it adds new information. It begins with the genealogy from Adam and continues through the patriarchs to David. The narrative starts in chapter 10 with the death of Saul. Chronicles takes us beyond the book of Kings, which ended with the destruction of Jerusalem by Babylon in 587 BC, and continues through to the Persian Empire in 539 BC and the decree of Cyrus allowing the people to return to Jerusalem. This time, we will read the books of the prophets at their appropriate place in the history.	
382. 1 Chronicles 1:1–54	382. Romans 5
383. 1 Chronicles 2:1–41	383. Romans 6
384. 1 Chronicles 2:42–3:24	384. Romans 7:1–13
385. 1 Chronicles 4	385. Romans 7:14–8:11
386. 1 Chronicles 5–6:30	386. Romans 8:12–27
387. 1 Chronicles 6:31–81	387. Romans 8:28–39
388. 1 Chronicles 7	388. Romans 9:1–18
389. 1 Chronicles 8–9:21	389. Romans 9:19–33
390. 1 Chronicles 9:22–10:14	390. Romans 10
391. 1 Chronicles 11	391. Romans 11:1–12
392. 1 Chronicles 12	392. Romans 11:13–24
393. 1 Chronicles 13–15	393. Romans 11:25–12:2
394. 1 Chronicles 16	394. Romans 12:3–21
395. 1 Chronicles 17–18	395. Romans 13
396. 1 Chronicles 19–20	396. Romans 14
397. 1 Chronicles 21–22:4	397. Romans 15:1–13
398. 1 Chronicles 22:5–23:32	398. Romans 15:14–33
399. 1 Chronicles 24–25	399. Romans 16:1–16
400. 1 Chronicles 26	400. Romans 16:17–27

	Paul left Macedonia and Greece with his companions, carrying the collection for the Christians in Judaea, and they arrived in Jerusalem in the year AD 59. The rest of the book of Acts deals with Paul's time in Jerusalem, his arrest, trial, appeal to Caesar (which was his legal right as a Roman citizen) and his turbulent journey to Rome, where we leave him under house arrest and awaiting his trial before Emperor Nero.
401. 1 Chronicles 27	401. Acts 21:1–16
402. 1 Chronicles 28–29:9	402. Acts 21:17–26
403. 1 Chronicles 29:10–30	403. Acts 21:27–39
At the death of King David we pause to read a cluster of **psalms**, some of which are from David himself. Those entitled 'A Song of Ascents' were used by the worshippers as they approached the tabernacle and later the temple in Jerusalem. Some, such as Psalm 126, which we have read before, were clearly written when the people returned from Persian exile after the decree of Cyrus in 539 BC.	
404. Psalms 101–103	404. Acts 21:40–22:21
405. Psalms 108–109	405. Acts 22:22–29
406. Psalms 110–112	406. Acts 22:30–23:11
407. Psalms 113–116	407. Acts 23:12–22
408. Psalms 117–118	408. Acts 23:23–35
409. Psalms 119:1–48	409. Acts 24
410. Psalms 119:49–96	410. Acts 25:1–12
411. Psalms 119:97–144	411. Acts 25:13–27
412. Psalms 119:145–176	412. Acts 26:1–18
413. Psalms 120–124	413. Acts 26:19–32
414. Psalms 125–129	414. Acts 27:1–12
415. Psalms 130–134	415. Acts 27:13–26
416. Psalms 135–136	416. Acts 27:27–44
From the reign of Solomon.	
417. 2 Chronicles 1–2:10	417. Acts 28:1–16
418. 2 Chronicles 2:11–4:22	418. Acts 28:17–31

	Ephesians, Colossians, Philemon and Philippians are Paul's letters from his house arrest in Rome. Some have suggested imprisonments in Ephesus and Caesarea, although Rome is the most generally accepted. This letter to the **Ephesians** is one of great encouragement, reminding the Christians that they are chosen and called by God, and loved and prayed for by Paul. He reminds them of their new life and union with Christ and emphasizes the gifts and essential unity in the church. The letter closes with instructions on practical Christian living: holiness, relationships and spiritual warfare.
419. 2 Chronicles 5–6:17	419. Ephesians 1
420. 2 Chronicles 6:18–7:10	420. Ephesians 2
421. 2 Chronicles 7:11–8:18	421. Ephesians 3
422. 2 Chronicles 9	422. Ephesians 4:1–16
423. 2 Chronicles 10–11:17	423. Ephesians 4:17–5:2
424. 2 Chronicles 11:18–14:1	424. Ephesians 5:3–33
425. 2 Chronicles 14:2–15:19	425. Ephesians 6
	The **Colossians** were in danger of being enticed by high-sounding philosophy; Paul reaffirms the true nature of Christ in some of the most descriptive phrases found in the New Testament. Typically of Paul, he closes with the pattern of Christian relationships and final greetings.
426. 2 Chronicles 16–17	426. Colossians 1:1–23
427. 2 Chronicles 18	427. Colossians 1:24–2:15
428. 2 Chronicles 19–20	428. Colossians 2:16–3:17
429. 2 Chronicles 21–22:9	429. Colossians 3:18–4:18
	Apparently the church at Colossae met in the home of Philemon, who was a wealthy Christian. One of his servants, Onesimus, had stolen from him, escaped to Rome, where he found the house Paul was renting, and become a Christian. Paul sends him back, accompanied by Tychicus, with this personal letter addressed to **Philemon**.
430. 2 Chronicles 22:10–23:21	430. Philemon

	Epaphroditus had brought gifts from the church at Philippi to support Paul, but had fallen seriously ill. When he recovered, Paul thought it wise to send him back to his home church as evidence of his return to health. Epaphroditus carried this letter with him. Paul writes to the **Philippians** of the humility and glory of Christ, the need for humility and unity in the church, the danger of false teaching and the need for holiness. He closes with his appreciation for their gifts and his usual final greetings.
431. 2 Chronicles 24	431. Philippians 1:1–14
The date of **Joel**'s preaching to Judah is uncertain, and therefore unnecessary. The most likely time is during the reign of Joash around 835 BC. He vividly describes judgement by a massive locust swarm but includes the promise of the coming Holy Spirit, fulfilled at Pentecost (Acts 2:16–21).	
432. Joel 1	432. Philippians 1:15–30
433. Joel 2:1–27	433. Philippians 2:1–18
434. Joel 2:28–3:21	434. Philippians 2:19–3:14
The reign of Amaziah of Judah which began in 796 BC.	
435. 2 Chronicles 25	435. Philippians 3:15–4:23
Amos was a contemporary of Isaiah and Hosea during the reigns of Uzziah of Judah and Jeroboam II of Israel, commencing around 780 BC. He warned Syria, on the northern border of Israel, of impending judgement, but directed most of his fire against Israel for their unfaithfulness.	The letters of Paul to Timothy and Titus are the last-recorded messages from Paul written shortly before his own martyrdom. He was now no longer under house arrest, but in prison. **Timothy** was a young worker sent to care for the church in Ephesus; Paul advises him how to establish a spiritual leadership in the church.
436. Amos 1–2	436. 1 Timothy 1:1–17
437. Amos 3–4	437. 1 Timothy 1:18–2:15
438. Amos 5–6	438. 1 Timothy 3
439. Amos 7–9	439. 1 Timothy 4

Isaiah preached during the reigns of Azariah (Uzziah), Jotham, Ahaz and Hezekiah. He was resident in Jerusalem at the time of Assyria's devastation of Judah in 701 BC. His prophecies are wide-ranging and include all Judah's neighbouring tribes and nations.	
440. Isaiah 1	440. 1 Timothy 5
441. Isaiah 2	441. 1 Timothy 6
	Here is Paul's final encouragement to **Timothy** to stand firm, together with an urgent request for Timothy to join him in Rome, bringing some personal items of Paul with him.
442. Isaiah 3–4	442. 2 Timothy 1
Our reading returns to the reign of Uzziah (Azariah) and Jotham of Judah.	
443. Isaiah 5:1–30	443. 2 Timothy 2
444. 2 Chronicles 26; Isaiah 6	444. 2 Timothy 3
445. 2 Chronicles 27:1–28:15	445. 2 Timothy 4
	Like Timothy, **Titus**, who was caring for the church in Crete, is given sound advice by Paul for the leadership and relationships within the church.
446. 2 Chronicles 28:16–27; Isaiah 7	446. Titus 1
Although warning of the impending invasion by Assyria, Isaiah looks beyond to the coming of the Messiah and the fulfilment of the promises of God.	
447. Isaiah 8–9:7	447. Titus 2
448. Isaiah 9:8–10:19	448. Titus 3
	John **Mark**, who failed as a young evangelist with Paul and then matured to become indispensable to the apostle (Acts 15:37–39; 2 Tim. 4:11), is generally accepted as the writer of this Gospel. An early record states that he worked with Peter, who guided the writing of this account of the life of Christ.
449. Isaiah 10:20–11:16	449. Mark 1:1–20
450. Isaiah 12–13	450. Mark 1:21–45
451. Isaiah 14:1–27	451. Mark 2:1–17

452. Isaiah 14:28–16:14	452. Mark 2:18–3:6
453. Isaiah 17–18	453. Mark 3:7–30
454. Isaiah 19	454. Mark 3:31–4:20
Hezekiah was a godly king whose reign enjoyed a spiritual revival. However, in his time Assyria devastated Judaea in the year 701 BC.	
455. 2 Chronicles 29	455. Mark 4:21–41
456. 2 Chronicles 30	456. Mark 5:1–20
457. 2 Chronicles 31–32:8	457. Mark 5:21–43
458. 2 Chronicles 32:9–33:25	458. Mark 6:1–13
We turn to a cluster of **psalms**, some by Asaph, who was David's lead musician and whose psalms were sung alongside David's in the time of Hezekiah (1 Chr. 16:4–5). However, the descendants of Asaph in the time of Hezekiah may be responsible for many of these.	
459. Psalms 73–74	459. Mark 6:14–29
460. Psalms 75–77	460. Mark 6:30–44
461. Psalm 78	461. Mark 6:45–56
462. Psalms 79–81	462. Mark 7:1–23
463. Psalms 82–84	463. Mark 7:24–37
464. Psalms 85–87	464. Mark 8:1–21
465. Psalms 88–89	465. Mark 8:22–9:1
As we saw, Isaiah was the resident prophet in Jerusalem during the reigns of Azariah (Uzziah), Jotham, Ahaz and Hezekiah. His book contains some of the greatest prophecies of the coming Messiah as well as following the narrative from Kings and Chronicles. Isaiah was preaching almost 150 years before Jeremiah, and, whereas the latter warned that the Babylonians would destroy the city, Isaiah reassured the people that Assyria would not so much as fire an arrow upon Jerusalem.	
466. Isaiah 20–21	466. Mark 9:2–13
467. Isaiah 22	467. Mark 9:14–32
468. Isaiah 23–24	468. Mark 9:33–50
469. Isaiah 25–26:11	469. Mark 10:1–16
470. Isaiah 26:12–27:13	470. Mark 10:17–34

471. Isaiah 28	471. Mark 10:35–52
472. Isaiah 29	472. Mark 11:1–19
473. Isaiah 30:1–26	473. Mark 11:20–33
474. Isaiah 30:27–32:8	474. Mark 12:1–17
475. Isaiah 32:9–33:16	475. Mark 12:18–34
476. Isaiah 33:17–34:17	476. Mark 12:35–44
477. Isaiah 35–36	477. Mark 13:1–23
478. Isaiah 37:1–29	478. Mark 13:24–14:11
479. Isaiah 37:30–39:8	479. Mark 14:12–31
480. Isaiah 40	480. Mark 14:32–52
481. Isaiah 41	481. Mark 14:53–72
482. Isaiah 42	482. Mark 15:1–20
483. Isaiah 43	483. Mark 15:21–41
484. Isaiah 44	484. Mark 15:42–16:20
	The last mention of **Peter** in the Acts of the Apostles is in chapter 15. Beyond there we cannot be certain of his movements as the focus is on Paul. This first letter was intended as a circular letter and not addressed to one church in particular. Possibly it was written from Rome, which may be coded as 'Babylon' in 5:13, and very likely before Paul's arrival in the city. It focuses on all that Christ achieved on the cross and prepares Christians scattered across the Roman Empire for the severe persecution that Peter knows is about to fall.
485. Isaiah 45	485. 1 Peter 1:1–12
486. Isaiah 46–47	486. 1 Peter 1:13–25
487. Isaiah 48	487. 1 Peter 2:1–12
488. Isaiah 49–50:9	488. 1 Peter 2:13–25
489. Isaiah 50:10–51:23	489. 1 Peter 3
490. Isaiah 52–53	490. 1 Peter 4
491. Isaiah 54–55	491. 1 Peter 5
	Peter warns against false teachers who are already invading the churches, and presents a clear statement of the uniqueness and authority of Scripture. This second letter closes on the positive theme of the promise of a new heavens and earth.
492. Isaiah 56–57:13	492. 2 Peter 1:1–11
493. Isaiah 57:14–58	493. 2 Peter 1:12–2:3

494. Isaiah 59	494. 2 Peter 2:4–22
495. Isaiah 60	495. 2 Peter 3
	Jude was a brother of our Lord and of the James who authored a letter and spoke persuasively at the Council in Jerusalem in Acts 15:13. Jude's short letter contains some of the strongest language against false teachers whose attacks against the person of Christ led to immoral behaviour. This is an indication that it was written later in the first century, when the heretical views and immoral practices of the Gnostics, who confused the simplicity of the historic gospel with strange ideas of inner light and secret knowledge, were gaining ground in many areas.
496. Isaiah 61–62	496. Jude 1–13
497. Isaiah 63	497. Jude 14–25
	The author of these three letters is almost certainly the disciple of Christ, the writer of the Gospel of John and of the final book of Revelation. Like Jude, **John** is clearly combatting early heresies of the Gnostics and those who denied the full deity and the real humanity of Christ, claiming that Jesus only 'seemed' to be God and man (known as Docetism).
498. Isaiah 64–65:16	498. 1 John 1
499. Isaiah 65:17–66:24	499. 1 John 2:1–14
Hosea was a contemporary of Isaiah and Amos. Like Amos, Hosea preached to Israel. He began preaching around 767 BC and continued through the reigns of Azariah (Uzziah), Jotham, Ahaz and Hezekiah of Judah and during the reign of Jeroboam II of Israel. The behaviour of his own promiscuous wife is seen as a tragic picture of Israel's unfaithfulness to their covenant God. Hosea warns of the final judgement on Israel which came in the year 722 BC with the Assyrian conquest.	
500. Hosea 1–2	500. 1 John 2:15–29

501. Hosea 3–4	501. 1 John 3
502. Hosea 5–6	502. 1 John 4
503. Hosea 7–8	503. 1 John 5
	It is a matter of debate whether the 'chosen lady' is a local church or some particular Christian lady. However, the value of this second letter does not depend on this identification. The themes are love, obedience, vigilance for the truth and resisting error.
504. Hosea 9–10	504. 2 John
	We cannot be certain who Gaius was, but this third letter is a warm commendation by the ageing apostle John and a serious warning against Diotrephes, who is spoiling the harmony of the fellowship.
505. Hosea 11–12	505. 3 John
	John's **revelation**, received while in exile on the isle of Patmos by order of the Emperor Diocletian, begins with a description of the risen and ascended Christ and letters addressed to seven churches across Asia Minor (modern-day Turkey). Then follows a vibrant declaration of the glory of Christ and his ultimate triumph over Satan and all the forces of evil. This is presented in a series of striking and vivid pictures. They repeat the same themes: the warfare of Christ and his church with evil in every form, the ultimate judgement of the devil and his followers, and the triumph of the church and its Saviour. Don't worry about the detail—enjoy the big picture. The history of the human race began in a garden with the tree of the knowledge of good and evil, and it closes in a garden in the new earth with the tree of life in the centre.
506. Hosea 13–14	506. Revelation 1

Micah was a contemporary of Hosea. His prophecy is radiant with the glory of the coming Messiah and redeemed church. The promises of the 'latter days' are to be taken as the time of the Messiah and not literal Israel.	
507. Micah 1–2:5	507. Revelation 2:1–11
508. Micah 2:6–3:12	508. Revelation 2:12–29
509. Micah 4	509. Revelation 3:1–13
510. Micah 5–6:8	510. Revelation 3:14–22
511. Micah 6:9–7:20	511. Revelation 4
The reign of the worst king of Judah, Manasseh, up to the destruction of Jerusalem and the temple by the Babylonian army of Nebuchadnezzar in 587 BC. Chronicles closes with a brief mention of the rise of the Persians to power when they captured Babylon in 539 BC.	
512. 2 Chronicles 33	512. Revelation 5
513. 2 Chronicles 34	513. Revelation 6
514. 2 Chronicles 35	514. Revelation 7
515. 2 Chronicles 36	515. Revelation 8
In spite of temporary reformation under the good King Josiah (640–609 BC), **Zephaniah**'s prophecy is one of foreboding because the people are not sincere.	
516. Zephaniah 1–2:12	516. Revelation 9
517. Zephaniah 2:13–3:20	517. Revelation 10
The prophet **Habakkuk** speaks of the rise of Babylon as something unimagined (1:5–11), which would place him in the time of Josiah before Babylon's defeat of Assyria (Nineveh) in 612 BC. After a dialogue with God, the prophet warns Babylon of her own eventual downfall.	
518. Habakkuk 1	518. Revelation 11
519 Habakkuk 2	519. Revelation 12
520 Habbakuk 3	520. Revelation 13
Ezra was a priest sent to Jerusalem in the time of Artaxerxes. He records the people who returned to Jerusalem after the decree of Cyrus in 539 BC.	

521. Ezra 1–2	521. Revelation 14
522. Ezra 3–4	522. Revelation 15
523. Ezra 5:1–6:12	523. Revelation 16
524. Ezra 6:13–7:28	524. Revelation 17
525. Ezra 8	525. Revelation 18:1–10
526. Ezra 9–10	526. Revelation 18:11–24
By September 520 BC the Jews had returned from exile and after a promising start to rebuild the temple they gave up in preference for their own houses. **Haggai** urged them back to work.	
527. Haggai 1–2	527. Revelation 19:1–10
Zechariah was a contemporary of Haggai. Eight visions are followed by promises of the coming Messiah and the triumph of his church.	
528. Zechariah 1–3	528. Revelation 19:11–21
529. Zechariah 4–7	529. Revelation 20
530. Zechariah 8–9	530. Revelation 21:1–14
531. Zechariah 10–12	531. Revelation 21:15–27
532. Zechariah 13–14	532. Revelation 22
Nehemiah, the cupbearer to the Persian King Artaxerxes, the son of Xerxes, became governor of Judaea at a crucial time of opposition to the rebuilding of the temple and the city walls.	This is our second reading of **Mark's Gospel**.
533. Nehemiah 1–2	533. Mark 1:1–20
534. Nehemiah 3	534. Mark 1:21–45
535. Nehemiah 4–5	535. Mark 2:1–17
536. Nehemiah 6–7	536. Mark 2:18–3:6
537. Nehemiah 8–9:5	537. Mark 3:7–30
538. Nehemiah 9:5–38	538. Mark 3:31–4:20
539. Nehemiah 10	539. Mark 4:21–41
540. Nehemiah 11–12:26	540. Mark 5:1–20
541. Nehemiah 12:27–13:31	541. Mark 5:21–43
Esther is the heroic account of one woman saving the Jewish people from genocide. Although God is never mentioned in this book, his providence is everywhere in focus. Esther was queen to Xerxes and therefore strictly her story precedes that of Nehemiah.	

542. Esther 1–2	542. Mark 6:1–13
543. Esther 3–4	543. Mark 6:14–29
544. Esther 5–7	544. Mark 6:30–44
545. Esther 8–10	545. Mark 6:45–56
Sometime after 423 BC and during the time of Nehemiah **Malachi** reminded the Jews how they were despising God's name and robbing him. He foretold the coming Elijah (John the Baptist) as the herald for the Messiah.	
546. Malachi 1–2	546. Mark 7:1–23
547. Malachi 3–4	547. Mark 7:24–37
Malachi closes the Old Testament around 400 BC. The years that follow are filled with the Persians who are defeated by the Greeks under Alexander the Great in 333 BC. The Egyptian Ptolemies were followed by the Syrian (Seleucid) dynasties and finally the Romans, whose legions first entered Palestine in 63 BC.	
The date of **Job** is unknown. It appears to be set in the age of the patriarchs, though its final written form may date to the time of Solomon. With good reason it is widely acknowledged as possibly the finest religious poem ever written. However, it is much more than this because it records the experience of a real man. The narrative faces up to the issue of suffering and both the wise and foolish responses to it. The sovereignty of God is at the heart of the whole debate.	
548. Job 1–2	548. Mark 8:1–30
549. Job 3–4	549. Mark 8:31–9:13
550. Job 5–6	550. Mark 9:14–32
551. Job 7–8	551. Mark 9:33–50
552. Job 9–10	552. Mark 10:1–16
553. Job 11–12	553. Mark 10:17–34
554. Job 13–14	554. Mark 10:35–52
555. Job 15–17	555. Mark 11:1–19
556. Job 18–19	556. Mark 11:20–33

557. Job 20–21	557. Mark 12:1–17
558 Job 22–23	558. Mark 12:18–34
559. Job 24–26	559. Mark 12:35–44
560. Job 27–28	560. Mark 13:1–23
561. Job 29–30	561. Mark 12:24–14:11
562. Job 31	562. Mark 14:12–31
563. Job 32–33	563. Mark 14:32–52
564. Job 34–35	564. Mark 14:53–72
565. Job 36–37	565. Mark 15:1–20
566. Job 38–39	566. Mark 15:21–41
567. Job 40–42	567. Mark 15:42–16:20

8. Take time with God

***Take time with God* can be downloaded as a PDF. Go to https://www.dayone.co.uk/collections/books/all-you-need-to-know**

Every morning lean your arms awhile
upon the windowsill of heaven
and gaze upon the Lord.
Then with the vision in your heart,
turn strong to meet your day.

The seventeenth-century Anglican minister Thomas Blake captured in this verse all that, a hundred years later, the American Congregational minister Austin Phelps referred to as 'The Still Hour' and which, a further hundred years on, was known by evangelical Christians as the 'Quiet Time'.

By whatever name it is known, the daily 'Time with God' has been lost in the busyness of the twenty-first century. In many Christian homes, husbands and wives do not pray together and children rarely hear their Christian parents pray at all. If prayers are offered, it is only occasionally and with as little time as we can manage to spare.

The rush of modern life is only one reason for the loss of what used to be an essential feature for every Christian home. We have lost an appetite for prayer because it is no longer seen as the privilege it really is: when a forgiven sinner can boldly approach the immediate presence of the Sovereign God of the universe and call him 'Father'. His ever-listening ear is always open for the voice of his children.

We have also lost confidence in prayer. So many of our prayers are seemingly unanswered. We do not get what we want or expect, so we give up. We agree with the importance of prayer, but leave it to others. Ours did not work, so why waste time?

There is another reason for our abandonment of 'Time with God'. We have so many things for which we should pray that we never quite get started. We may have tried schemes without number, but they all come to nothing sooner or later.

Planned praying is rejected as unspiritual by some Christians, so they are content either not to pray at all or to enter the shallows of prayers that wander around until the mind drifts away.

If the essentials for a healthy Christian life—time with God's word and time with God himself—are not to be lost altogether, we must reassess their importance in our life and make time for them. But we must do more than make time. We must make both our reading and our praying meaningful.

What follows here is only a guide to keep us focused each day. It will ensure that we do not rush into prayer and badger God with a long list of requests before we have settled our minds on the God we are approaching. An adoring, thankful and repentant heart is what God desires from his people before they come with supplication and intercession.

We must each turn the guide here into our own 'Time with God'. The suggested headings need to be filled out with our personal items for thanksgiving and intercession. There are reliable Christian missions that provide daily prayer guides for persecuted Christians. We cannot pray for everything and everyone each day, but over the course of a week we can bring before God many of those people and concerns that we have often promised to pray for.

The Scripture verses are intended to root our prayers in the word of God. And there can be no more persuasive prayers with God than those that are based upon his promise and pattern. Some of the deepest and strongest prayers ever written come from the hand of the apostle Paul, so we have taken one of these each day and turned it to our own use.

Our 'Time with God' and his word is intended to be an enjoyable privilege. Let's make it so.

Sunday

ADORATION

For God in creation

'Who has measured the waters in the hollow of his hand, or with the breadth of his hand marked off the heavens? Who has held the dust of the earth in a basket, or weighed the mountains on the scales and the hills in a balance? Who has understood the mind of the LORD, or instructed him as his counsellor? Whom did the LORD consult to enlighten him, and who taught him the right way? Who was it that taught him knowledge or showed him the path of understanding?' Isaiah 40:12–14).

CONFESSION

'Jesus replied: "'Love the Lord your God with all your heart and with all your soul and with all your mind.' This is the first and greatest commandment. And the second is like it: 'Love your neighbour as yourself'"' (Matthew 22:37–39).

THANKSGIVING

For the Lord's day

'By the seventh day God had finished the work he had been doing; so on the seventh day he rested from all his work. And God blessed the seventh day and made it holy, because on it he rested from all the work of creating that he had done' Genesis 2:2–3).

For our home and family

'As for me and my household, we will serve the Lord' (Joshua 24:15).

For preaching and Christian fellowship

'I always pray with joy because of your partnership in the gospel from the first day until now' (Philippians 1:4–5).

SUPPLICATION

For ourselves, our family and our church

We pray that out of your glorious riches you will strengthen us with power through your Spirit in our inner being, so that Christ may dwell in our hearts through faith. And we pray that, being rooted and established in love, we may have power, together with all the saints, to grasp how wide and long and high and deep is the love of Christ, and to know this love that surpasses knowledge—that we may be filled to the measure of all the fullness of God (based on Ephesians 3:16–19).

For preachers to preach with attractive and Holy Spirit power

'My message and my preaching were not with wise and persuasive words, but with a demonstration of the Spirit's power, so that your faith might not rest on men's wisdom, but on God's power' (1 Corinthians 2:4–5).

For revival

'Although our sins testify against us, O LORD, do something for the sake of your name. For our backsliding is great; we have sinned against you ... O LORD, we acknowledge our wickedness and the guilt of our fathers; we have indeed sinned against you. For the sake of your name do not despise us; do not dishonour your glorious throne. Remember your covenant with us and do not break it' (Jeremiah 14:7, 20–21).

INTERCESSION FOR OTHERS

For persecuted Christians

'Remember those in prison as if you were their fellow-prisoners, and those who are ill-treated as if you yourselves were suffering' (Hebrews 13:3).

For our missionary friends and missions

'Pray for us that the message of the Lord may spread rapidly and be honoured ... And pray that we may be delivered from wicked and evil men, for not everyone has faith' (2 Thessalonians 3:1–2).

For our church leaders and members

'Respect those who ... are over you in the Lord ... Hold them in the highest regard in love because of their work. Live in peace with each other' (1 Thessalonians 5:12–13).

Monday

ADORATION

For the providence of God

'Oh, the depth of the riches of the wisdom and knowledge of God! How unsearchable his judgments, and his paths beyond tracing out! Who has known the mind of the Lord? Or who has been his counsellor? Who has ever given to God, that God should repay him? For from him and through him and to him are all things. To him be the glory for ever! Amen' (Romans 11:33–36).

CONFESSION

'Do not let any unwholesome talk come out of your mouths, but only what is helpful for building others up according to their needs, that it may benefit those who listen. And do not grieve the Holy Spirit of God, with whom you were sealed for the day of redemption' (Ephesians 4:29–30).

THANKSGIVING

For our home and family

'No good thing does [God] withhold from those whose walk is blameless' (Psalm 84:11).

For God's love and forgiveness

'The LORD is compassionate and gracious, slow to anger, abounding in love ... He does not treat us as our sins deserve or repay us according to our iniquities. For as high as the heavens are above the earth, so great is his love for those who fear him; as far as the east is from the west, so far has he removed our transgressions from us. As a father has compassion on his children, so the LORD has compassion on those who fear him' (Psalm 103:8, 10–13).

For his Holy Spirit and the Bible

'All Scripture is God-breathed and is useful for teaching, rebuking, correcting and training in righteousness, so that the man of God may be thoroughly equipped for every good work' (2 Timothy 3:16–17).

SUPPLICATION

For ourselves, our family and our church

O God who gives endurance and encouragement, give us a spirit of unity among ourselves as we follow Christ Jesus, so that with one heart and mouth we may glorify you, the God and Father of our Lord Jesus Christ. Fill us with all joy and peace as we trust in you, so that we may overflow with hope by the power of the Holy Spirit (based on Romans 15:5–6, 13).

For true wisdom from God

'But the wisdom that comes from heaven is first of all pure; then peace-loving, considerate, submissive, full of mercy and good fruit, impartial and sincere. Peacemakers who sow in peace raise a harvest of righteousness' (James 3:17–18).

For revival

'If my people, who are called by my name, will humble themselves and pray and seek my face and turn from their wicked ways, then will I hear from heaven and will forgive their sin and will heal their land' (2 Chronicles 7:14).

INTERCESSION FOR OTHERS

For persecuted Christians

'For a little while you may have had to suffer grief in all kinds of trials … so that your faith—of greater worth than gold, which perishes even though refined by fire—may be proved genuine and may result in praise, glory and honour when Jesus Christ is revealed' (1 Peter 1:6–7).

For our friends

'A friend loves at all times, and a brother is born for adversity' (Proverbs 17:17).

For Christians involved in education

'A student is not above his teacher, but everyone who is fully trained will be like his teacher' (Luke 6:40).

For the moral and spiritual life of our nation

'Seek the peace and prosperity of the city to which I have carried you … Pray to the LORD for it, because if it prospers, you too will prosper' (Jeremiah 29:7).

Tuesday

ADORATION

For the glory of God

'All the angels were standing round the throne and around the elders and the four living creatures. They fell down on their faces before the throne and worshipped God, saying: "Amen! Praise and glory and wisdom and thanks and honour and power and strength be to our God for ever and ever. Amen!"' (Revelation 7:11–12).

For God's faithfulness

'Know therefore that the LORD your God is God; he is the faithful God, keeping his covenant of love to a thousand generations of those who love him and keep his commands' (Deuteronomy 7:9).

CONFESSION

'I have strayed like a lost sheep. Seek your servant, for I have not forgotten your commands' (Psalm 119:176).

THANKSGIVING

For our health and God's provision of many good things

'Command those who are rich in this present world not to be arrogant nor to put their hope in wealth, which is so uncertain, but to put their hope in God, who richly provides us with everything for our enjoyment' (1 Timothy 6:17).

For assurance of salvation

'I am convinced that neither death nor life, neither angels nor demons, neither the present nor the future, nor any powers, neither height nor depth, nor anything else in all creation, will be able to separate us from the love of God that is in Christ Jesus our Lord' (Romans 8:38–39).

SUPPLICATION

For ourselves, our family and our church

O God of our Lord Jesus Christ, our glorious Father, we pray that you will give us the Spirit of wisdom and revelation, so that we may know you better. We pray also that the eyes of our hearts may be enlightened in order that we may know the hope to which you have called us, the riches of your glorious inheritance in the saints, and your incomparably great power for us who believe (based on Ephesians 1:17–19).

To be filled with the fruit of the Spirit

'The fruit of the Spirit is love, joy, peace, patience, kindness, goodness, faithfulness, gentleness and self-control ... Those who belong to Christ Jesus have crucified the sinful nature with its passions and desires. Since we live by the Spirit, let us keep in step with the Spirit' (Galatians 5:22–25).

For opportunity to witness and the wise use of time

'Be very careful, then, how you live—not as unwise but as wise, making the most of every opportunity, because the days are evil' (Ephesians 5:15–16).

For revival

'We have heard with our ears, O God; our fathers have told us what you did in their days, in days long ago ... You have made us a reproach to our neighbours, the scorn and derision of those around us. You have made us a byword among the nations; the peoples shake their heads at us ... Awake, O Lord! Why do you sleep? Rouse yourself! Do not reject us for ever. Why do you hide your face and forget our misery and oppression? ... Rise up and help us; redeem us because of your unfailing love' (Psalm 44:1, 13–14, 23–24, 26).

INTERCESSION FOR OTHERS

For persecuted Christians

'Consider him who endured such opposition from sinful men, so that you will not grow weary and lose heart' (Hebrews 12:3).

For Christians at work

'Whatever you do ... do it all in the name of the Lord Jesus, giving thanks to God the Father through him ... work at it with all your heart, as working for the Lord, not for men' (Colossians 3:17, 23).

For the elderly, all who are unwell mentally or physically, and those who care for them

'Even to your old age and grey hairs I am he, I am he who will sustain you. I have made you and I will carry you; I will sustain you and I will rescue you' (Isaiah 46:4).

Wednesday

ADORATION

For God's love and faithfulness

'Your love, O LORD, reaches to the heavens, your faithfulness to the skies. Your righteousness is like the mighty mountains, your justice like the great deep. O LORD, you preserve both man and beast. How priceless is your unfailing love! Both high and low among men find refuge in the shadow of your wings' (Psalm 36:5–7).

CONFESSION

'... According to your great compassion blot out my transgressions. Wash away all my iniquity and cleanse me from my sin. For I know my transgressions, and my sin is always before me. Against you, you only, have I sinned and done what is evil in your sight' (Psalm 51:1–4).

THANKSGIVING

For our home and family

'[Cornelius] and all his family were devout and God-fearing; he gave generously to those in need and prayed to God regularly' (Acts 10:2).

For freedom and peace

'The LORD is a refuge for the oppressed, a stronghold in times of trouble' (Psalm 9:9).

For the intercession of Christ

'We have a great high priest who has gone through the heavens, Jesus the Son of God ... We have one who has been tempted in every way, just as we are—yet was without sin. Let us then approach the throne of grace with confidence, so that we may receive mercy and find grace to help us in our time of need' (Hebrews 4:14–16).

SUPPLICATION

For ourselves, our family and our church

Lord, fill us with the knowledge of your will through all spiritual wisdom and understanding, in order that we may live lives worthy of you and may please you in every way. Help us to bear fruit in every good work and to grow in the knowledge of God. Strengthen us with all power according to your glorious might so that we may have great endurance and patience, and joyfully give thanks to you, who have qualified us to share in the inheritance of the saints in the kingdom of light (based on Colossians 1:9–12).

To be strong in Christ

'Be strong in the Lord and in his mighty power. Put on the full armour of God so that you can take your stand against the devil's schemes ... And pray in the Spirit on all occasions with all kinds of prayers and requests. With this in mind, be alert and always keep on praying for all the saints' (Ephesians 6:10–11, 18).

For revival

'"Has God forgotten to be merciful? Has he in anger withheld his compassion?" Then I thought, "To this I will appeal: the years of the right hand of the Most High." I will remember the deeds of the LORD; yes, I will remember your miracles of long ago. I will meditate on all your works and consider all your mighty deeds. Your ways, O God, are holy. What god is so great as our God? You are the God who performs miracles; you display your power among the peoples' (Psalm 77:9–14).

INTERCESSION FOR OTHERS

For persecuted Christians

'Consider it pure joy, my brothers, whenever you face trials of many kinds, because you know that the testing of your faith develops perseverance' (James 1:2–3).

For singles and those bereaved

'If you have any encouragement from being united with Christ, if any comfort from his love, if any fellowship with the Spirit, if any tenderness and compassion, then make my joy complete by being like-minded, having the same love, being one in spirit and purpose' (Philippians 2:1–2).

For Christian parents

'Train a child in the way he should go, and when he is old he will not turn from it' (Proverbs 22:6).

Thursday

ADORATION

The Triune God and his electing love

'[You have been] chosen according to the foreknowledge of God the Father, through the sanctifying work of the Spirit, for obedience to Jesus Christ and sprinkling by his blood ... Praise be to the God and Father of our Lord Jesus Christ! In his great mercy he has given us new birth into a living hope through the resurrection of Jesus Christ from the dead, and into an inheritance that can never perish, spoil or fade—kept in heaven for you' (1 Peter 1:2–4).

CONFESSION

'He who conceals his sins does not prosper, but whoever confesses and renounces them finds mercy' (Proverbs 28:13; see also 6:16–19).

THANKSGIVING

For the privilege of being a Christian

'To all who received him, to those who believed in his name, he gave the right to become children of God' (John 1:12).

For God's promises

'Through [God's goodness and glory] he has given us his very great and precious promises, so that through them you may participate in the divine nature and escape the corruption in the world caused by evil desires' (2 Peter 1: 4).

For the certain hope of Christ's return

'... We wait for the blessed hope—the glorious appearing of our great God and Saviour, Jesus Christ' (Titus 2:13).

SUPPLICATION

For ourselves, our family and our church

Lord, we pray that you may count us worthy of your calling, and that by your power you will fulfil every good purpose of ours and every act prompted by our faith. We pray this so that the name of our Lord Jesus may be glorified in us, and we in him, according to the grace of our God and the Lord Jesus Christ (based on 2 Thessalonians 1:11–12).

To be kept pure

'For God did not call us to be impure, but to live a holy life' (1 Thessalonians 4:7).

To be humble in assessing others

'So then, each of us will give an account of himself to God. Therefore let us stop passing judgment on one another. Instead, make up your mind not to put any stumbling-block or obstacle in your brother's way' (Romans 14:12–13).

For revival

'Restore us again, O God our Saviour, and put away your displeasure towards us. Will you be angry with us for ever? Will you prolong your anger through all generations? Will you not revive us again, that your people may rejoice in you? Show us your unfailing love, O LORD, and grant us your salvation ... The LORD will indeed give what is good, and our land will yield its harvest. Righteousness goes before him and prepares the way for his steps' (Psalm 85:4–7, 12–13).

INTERCESSION FOR OTHERS

For persecuted Christians

'If you suffer as a Christian, do not be ashamed, but praise God that you bear that name' (1 Peter 4:16).

For unsaved relatives, friends, neighbours and colleagues

'The Lord is ... patient with you, not wanting anyone to perish, but everyone to come to repentance' (2 Peter 3:9).

For those in the police and security forces

'He has delivered us from such a deadly peril, and he will deliver us. On him we have set our hope that he will continue to deliver us' (2 Corinthians 1:10).

Friday

ADORATION

For the power of God

'Sing to God, O kingdoms of the earth, sing praise to the Lord, to him who rides the ancient skies above, who thunders with mighty voice. Proclaim the power of God, whose majesty is over Israel, whose power is in the skies. You are awesome, O God, in your sanctuary; the God of Israel gives power and strength to his people. Praise be to God!' (Psalm 68:32–35).

For the presence of God

'O LORD, you have searched me and you know me. You know when I sit and when I rise; you perceive my thoughts from afar. You discern my going out and my lying down; you are familiar with all my ways. Before a word is on my tongue you know it completely, O LORD. You hem me in—behind and before; you have laid your hand upon me. Such knowledge is too wonderful for me, too lofty for me to attain. Where can I go from your Spirit? Where can I flee from your presence?' (Psalm 139:1–7).

CONFESSION

'But if you harbour bitter envy and selfish ambition in your hearts, do not boast about it or deny the truth. Such "wisdom" does not come down from heaven but is earthly, unspiritual, of the devil. For where you have envy and selfish ambition, there you find disorder and every evil practice' (James 3:14–16).

THANKSGIVING

For our home and family

'... Rejoice in all the good things the LORD your God has given to you and your household' (Deuteronomy 26:11).

For the peace of God

'... And the peace of God, which transcends all understanding, will guard your hearts and your minds in Christ Jesus' (Philippians 4:7).

For the love of God

'How great is the love the Father has lavished on us, that we should be called children of God!' (1 John 3:1).

SUPPLICATION

For ourselves, our family and our church

Lord, may our love abound more and more in knowledge and depth of insight, so that we may be able to discern what is best and may be pure and blameless until the day of Christ, filled with the fruit of righteousness that comes through Jesus Christ, to your glory and praise (based on Philippians 1:9–11).

To cultivate a Christian character

'Make every effort to add to your faith goodness; and to goodness, knowledge; and to knowledge, self-control; and to self-control, perseverance; and to perseverance, godliness; and to godliness, brotherly kindness; and to brotherly kindness, love' (2 Peter 1:5–7).

For revival

'Oh, that you would rend the heavens and come down ... to make your name known to your enemies and cause the nations to quake before you! ... Since ancient times no one has heard, no ear has perceived, no eye has seen any God besides you, who acts on behalf of those who wait for him. You come to the help of those who gladly do right, who remember your ways' (Isaiah 64:1–2, 4–5).

INTERCESSION FOR OTHERS

For persecuted Christians

'Those who suffer according to God's will should commit themselves to their faithful Creator and continue to do good' (1 Peter 4:19).

For evangelism across the nation

'Devote yourselves to prayer, being watchful and thankful ... that God may open a door for our message' (Colossians 4:2–3).

For leaders in national and local government

'I urge, then, first of all, that requests, prayers, intercession and thanksgiving be made for everyone—for kings and all those in authority, that we may live peaceful and quiet lives in all godliness and holiness' (1 Timothy 2:1–2).

Saturday

ADORATION

For the holiness of God

'I saw the Lord seated on a throne, high and exalted, and the train of his robe filled the temple. Above him were seraphs, each with six wings: With two wings they covered their faces, with two they covered their feet, and with two they were flying. And they were calling to one another: "Holy, holy, holy is the LORD Almighty; the whole earth is full of his glory" ' (Isaiah 6:1–3).

CONFESSION

'You have set our iniquities before you, our secret sins in the light of your presence' (Psalm 90:8).

THANKSGIVING

For the word of God in the Bible

'Your word is a lamp to my feet and a light for my path' (Psalm 119:105).

For the hope of heaven

'... We wait for the blessed hope—the glorious appearing of our great God and Saviour, Jesus Christ' (Titus 2:13).

For the universal and local church

'All over the world this gospel is bearing fruit and growing' (Colossians 1:6).

SUPPLICATION

For ourselves, our family and our church

May you yourself, the God of peace, sanctify us through and through. May our whole spirit, soul and body be kept blameless at the coming of our Lord Jesus Christ (based on 1 Thessalonians 5:23).

To be wise and generous in giving

'Give, and it will be given to you. A good measure, pressed down, shaken together and running over, will be poured into your lap. For with the measure you use, it will be measured to you' (Luke 6:38).

For revival

'I will pour water on the thirsty land, and streams on the dry ground; I will pour out my Spirit on your offspring, and my blessing on your descendants. They will spring up like grass in a meadow, like poplar trees by flowing streams. One will say, "I belong to the LORD"; another will call himself by the name of Jacob; still another will write on his hand, "The LORD's", and will take the name Israel' (Isaiah 44:3–5).

INTERCESSION FOR OTHERS

For persecuted Christians

'When you pass through the waters, I will be with you … When you walk through the fire, you will not be burned; the flames will not set you ablaze. For I am the LORD, your God, the Holy One of Israel, your Saviour' (Isaiah 43:2–3).

For evangelism in prisons across our country

'If anyone is in Christ, he is a new creation; the old has gone, the new has come! All this is from God, who reconciled us to himself through Christ and gave us the ministry of reconciliation' (2 Corinthians 5:17–18).

For churches known to us

'I will build my church, and the gates of Hades will not overcome it' (Matthew 16:18).

For those preparing for ministry

'Pray for us … that we may proclaim the mystery of Christ … clearly', 'in truthful speech and in the power of God' (Colossians 4:3–4; 2 Corinthians 6:7).

Index to significant subjects

These references will take the reader only to the book and chapter (eg 1/3, 4/5) in this series where the more significant references to the subject occur.

Index to main Scripture references

These references will take the reader only to the book and chapter (eg 1/3, 4/5) in this series where the more significant Scripture references occur.

Additional commendations

'*All you need to know about the Bible* blends apologetics, history and biblical studies to produce this important and hugely enjoyable series. It provides the reader with a mental landscape within which a confident and intelligent love for the Bible can be nurtured. It is a tour de force and a marvellous gift to the church in our secular age. I could not commend it more warmly or enthusiastically.'

RICHARD CUNNINGHAM,
Director, Universities and Colleges Christian Unions

'Accessible throughout, these comprehensive introductory accounts of Scripture will be of immense value to everyone who reads them. They go far beyond a simple introduction and probe deeply into the nature of the Bible as the faultless Word of God, considering and answering a full range of criticisms. Moreover, Brian writes in a manner that will benefit the newest Christian. I hope his work receives the widest possible readership.'

DR ROBERT LETHAM, *Professor of Systematic and Historical Theology, Union School of Theology, Wales*

'The overwhelming strength of Brian's comprehensive series is that it provides ordinary Christians with confidence in the authority of the Bible. Brian has the skill to make this subject accessible without simplification or omission. What a great resource for Christians, equipping us to be on the front foot when it comes to defending the Bible against its many detractors!'

ADRIAN REYNOLDS,
author, local church pastor and Training Director of the Fellowship of Independent Evangelical Churches

---

'Each one of these books is a valuable guide to the teaching and historical reliability of the Bible. Together, the set builds a compelling case for the authority of Scripture as the very words of God with life-changing power. A wealth of material in readable style, it is a rich resource, giving fresh confidence in the reliability and authority of the Scriptures.'

BILL JAMES,
Principal, The London Seminary
